KB263445

FLAT STANLEY

Stanley, Flat Again!

Stanley, Flat Again!

Text copyright © 2003 by Jeff Brown
Illustrations by Macky Pamintuan, copyright © 2009 by HarperCollins Publishers
All rights reserved.

No part of this publication may be reproduced, stored in a retrieval system, or transmitted, in any form or by any means, graphic, electronic, or mechanical, including photocopying, taping, and recording, without prior written permission from the publisher.
For information about permission, write to editor@ltinc.net

Published in agreement with the author, c/o BAROR INTERNATIONAL, INC., Armonk, New York, U.S.A. through Danny Hong Agency, Seoul, Korea.

ISBN 979-11-93992-42-5 14740

Longtail Books

이 책의 저작권은 저자와의 계약으로 롱테일북스에 있습니다.
저작권법에 의해 한국 내에서 보호를 받는 저작물이므로 무단 전재와 복제를 금합니다.

FLAT STANLEY

Stanley, Flat Again!

by Jeff Brown
Pictures by Macky Pamintuan

For Peter and Wendy,
Ozinger, Betsy, and Ash

CONTENTS

SPORTS
CHAMPS!
34

A Morning Surprise

Mrs. Lambchop was making breakfast. Mr. Lambchop, at the kitchen table, helped by reading **bit**s from the morning paper.

"Here's an **odd** one, Harriet," he said. "There's a chicken in Sweden that rides a bike."

"So do I, George," said Mrs. Lambchop, not really listening.

"Listen to this. 'Merker Building **emptied**. To be **collapse**d next week.' **Imagine**! Eight floors!"

"Poor thing!" Mrs. Lambchop **set out plate**s. "Boys!" she called. "Breakfast is ready!"

Her **glance** fell upon a **row** of photographs on the wall above the **sink**. There was a smiling Stanley, only half an inch* thick, his big **bulletin board** having fallen from the bedroom wall to **rest** upon him **overnight**. Next came **remind**ers of the many family **adventure**s that had come after Stanley's younger brother, Arthur, had **clever**ly blown him round

---

★ **inch** 길이의 단위 인치. 1인치는 약 2.54센티미터이다.

again with a bicycle **pump**. There were
the brothers with Prince Haraz, the young
genie* who had **grant**ed wishes for them
all after being **accidental**ly **summon**ed by
Stanley from a lamp. There was the entire
family with Santa Claus and his daughter,
Sarah, taken during a Christmas visit
to the North **Pole**. There was the family
again in Washington, D.C.,* in the office
of the **President** of the United States, who
had asked them to **undertake** a secret
mission into **outer space**. The last picture
showed Arthur standing beside a balloon
on which Mrs. Lambchop had painted a

★ **genie** 지니. 아라비아 신화에서 병이나 램프 속에 사는 요정.
✳ **Washington, D.C.** 미국의 수도 워싱턴 D.C.

picture of Stanley's face. The balloon, its **string** in fact held by Stanley, had been a **valuable** guide to his **presence**, since he was in**visible** at the time. "Boys!" she called again. "Breakfast!"

In their bedroom, Stanley and Arthur had finished **dress**ing.

While Stanley filled his **backpack**, Arthur **bounce**d a tennis ball. "Let's go," he said. "Here! Catch!"

Stanley had just **reach**ed for a book on the **shelf** by his bed. The ball **struck** his back as he turned, and he **bang**ed his shoulder on a corner of the shelf.

"**Ouch!**"

★ **boy** 여기에서는 '소년'이라는 뜻이 아니라, 놀람·기쁨·아픔 등을 나타내는 '맙소사!', '어머나!'라는 의미로 쓰였다.

"Sorry," Arthur said. "But let's go, okay? You know how long—STANLEY!"

"Why are you shouting?" Stanley **adjust**ed his pack. "C'mon! I'm so hungry—" He **pause**d. "Oh, boy!* Arthur, do you see?"

"I do, actually." Arthur **swallow**ed

hard. "You're, you know . . . flat."

The brothers **stare**d at each other.

"The pump?" Stanley said. "It might work again."

Arthur **fetch**ed the bicycle pump from their toy **chest**, and Stanley lay on his bed with the **hose** end in his mouth.

Arthur gave a long, **steady**, pump.

Stanley **made a face**. "That hurts!"

Arthur pumped again, and Stanley **snatch**ed the hose from his mouth. "Owww! That really hurts! It wasn't like that before. We'd better stop."

"Now what?" Arthur said. "We can't just hide in here forever, you know."

Mrs. Lambchop's call came again. "Boys! Please come!"

"Do me a **favor**," Stanley said. "You tell them. Sort of get them ready, okay?"

"Okay," said Arthur, and went to tell.

* * *

Arthur stood in the kitchen **doorway**. "Hey, guess what?" he said.

"**Hay** is for horses, **dear**," said Mrs. Lambchop. "Good morning! Breakfast is ready."

"Good morning, Arthur," Mr. Lambchop said from behind his newspaper. "Where's Stanley?"

"Guess what?" Arthur said again.

Mrs. Lambchop **sigh**ed. "Oh, all right! I can't guess. Tell."

"Stanley's flat again," said Arthur.

Mr. Lambchop put down his paper.

Mrs. Lambchop closed her eyes. "Flat again? Is that what you said?"

"Yes," said Arthur.

"It's true." Stanley stood now beside Arthur in the doorway. "Just look."

"**Good grief**!" said Mr. Lambchop. "I can't believe that bulletin board—"

"It didn't fall on me this time," Stanley said. "I just got flat. Arthur tried to pump me up, like before, but it hurt too much."

"Oh, Stanley!" Mrs. Lambchop ran to kiss him. "How do you feel now?"

"Fine, actually," Stanley said. "Just surprised. Can I go to school?"

Mrs. Lambchop thought for a moment. "Very well. Eat your breakfast. After school we'll hear what Dr. Dan has to say."

Dr. Dan

"Ah, Mr. and Mrs. Lambchop! And the boys!" said Dr. Dan as they entered his office. "How nice to—"

His eyes **widen**ed. **"Good heavens,** Stanley! Mr. Lambchop, you really must do something about that **bulletin board!"**

"It is still **firm**ly in place, Dr. Dan," Mrs. Lambchop said. "We **are at a loss** to

account for this **attack** of flatness."

"Hmmm." Dr. Dan thought for a moment. "Is there, perhaps, a family history of flatness?"

"No," Mr. Lambchop said. "We'd remember that."

"We got **dress**ed for school," Stanley explained. "We didn't even have breakfast. And **all of a sudden**, I got flat."

Dr. Dan **frown**ed. "Nothing happened? Nothing at all?"

"Well, Arthur **hit** me with a tennis ball," Stanley said. "And then I **bang**ed my shoulder on—"

"Aha!" Jumping up, Dr. Dan took a large book from the **case** behind his desk and began turning pages. "This is Dr.

Franz Gemeister's excellent *Difficult and Peculiar Cases*. Just let me find . . . here it is! 'Flatness, page two seventeen!'"

He read aloud. "'Sudden flatness . . . **extreme**ly **rare** . . . **minimal documentation** . . . **hearsay report**s . . .' Ah, here it is!

Dates back to the fifth **century**! 'During

battle, Mongo the **Fierce**, an **aide** to

Attila* the Hun,* was **struck** twice,

simultaneously, from behind, and **at once**

became no thicker than his **shield**. He became known as Mongo the **Plate**, and lived to old age without **regain**ing his original **girth**.'"

Dr. Dan closed the book. "As I **suspect**ed! The OBP."

"**Beg pardon**?" said Mrs. Lambchop.

"The OBP. **Osteal** Balance Point," Dr. Dan explained. "A little-known **anatomical feature**. The human body, of course, is a **complex miracle**, its **skeleton** a **delicate framework** of **support**s and balances. The Osteal Balance Point may **occur** almost anywhere in the upper **torso**. It

----

★ **Attila** 아틸라. 훈족의 왕. 5세기 전반에 유럽에 침입하고 주변의 게르만족과 동고트족 등을 굴복시켜 대제국을 건설하였다.

✳ **the Hun** 훈족. 중앙아시아의 스텝 지대에 거주했던 투르크계의 유목기마 민족.

is **vulnerable** only to the **application** of simultaneous **pressure**s at two points which **vary depend**ing on the age and **particular 'design,' let us say**, of the **individual involve**d. In my opinion, the pressures created by the tennis ball and the **shelf** corner **affect**ed Stanley's OBP, **thereby** turning him flat."

For a moment, everyone was silent.

"The first time Stanley went flat, you were greatly **puzzle**d by his condition," Mr. Lambchop said at last. "Now you seem **remarkably** well **inform**ed."

"I **read up on** it," said Dr. Dan.

Mrs. Lambchop **sigh**ed. "Perhaps we should **seek** a second opinion. Who is the world's **leading authority** on the OBP?"

"That would be me," said Dr. Dan.

"I see. . . . Well, we've taken enough of your time." Mr. Lambchop rose, **motion**ing his family to follow. "Thank you, Dr. Dan."

At the door, Mrs. Lambchop turned. "Perhaps if we found the, you know, the OBP, we could make Stanley—"

"No, no!" said Dr. Dan. "It would be dangerous to **put** the **lad through** such a **skeletal strain** again! And finding the OBP? Not very likely, I'm afraid."

Arthur had an idea. "I know! If we all got **stick**s and hit Stanley all over at the same time, and kept doing it, then—"

"That will do, Arthur," Mr. Lambchop said, and led his family out.

Stanley Sails

Early the next Sunday morning, Mr. Lambchop had a call from an old **college** friend, Ralph Jones.

"Just wanted to **remind** you, George, that Stanley and I have a **date** to go sailing today," he said.

"He's looking forward to it, Ralph." Mr. Lambchop **hesitated**. "I should **mention**, perhaps, that Stanley has gone flat again."

Mr. Jones sighed. "I thought he'd **got over** that. Well, I'll **pick** him **up** at ten."

Later that morning, driving with Stanley to his sailing club on the **seashore**, Mr. Jones **inquire**d about a **foreign** visitor he had once met with the Lambchops. "A prince, yes? He around these days?"

Stanley knew he meant the young genie, Prince Haraz, but it would be difficult to explain not only the genie part, but also that Haraz had returned to the genie **kingdom** from which he had come.

"No," Stanley said. "He went home, actually."

"Too bad." Mr. Jones was famous for his **amazing** memory. "Haraz, as I **recall**.

Prince Fawzi Mustafa Aslan Mirza Malek Namerd Haraz?"

"Right," said Stanley.

In the **harbor** of the sailing club, Mr. Jones prepared his boat, *Lovebug*, and explained it to Stanley. "This big sail here is the mainsail,* and that's the **rudder** back there, for **steer**ing. In this **zip** bag is another sail, called a spinnaker.* We'll use that one for extra speed when we're **run**ning **before the wind**. See that boat way out there, how its spinnaker is **puff**ing out front?"

Stanley laughed. The spinnaker looked

★ **mainsail** 주범. 배의 돛들 중 제일 크고 중요한 돛.
✳ **spinnaker** 스피나커. 경주용 요트에 추가로 다는 큰 삼각형 모양의 돛. 많은 양의 바람을 잡아 배의 속도를 증가시킨다.

like an open umbrella lying on its side.

"See over there," Mr. Jones **went on**, "between the **committee** boat, with the **judge**s on it, and the red **buoy**? That's the starting line. The **race** ends back there too. First boat to cross that line wins!"

He **cast** off the **moor**ing line, and the mainsail filled. *Lovebug* headed out to join the other boats.

Mr. Jones pointed. "There! That's Jasper Green's boat, *Windswept*. He's the one I want especially to **beat**!"

"Why? Are you mad at him?" Stanley asked.

"He was very rude to me once. But **never mind**. Let's just make sure we win!"

Behind the start line, they found themselves beside *Windswept*. Jasper Green gave a **friendly wave**, but Ralph Jones **ignore**d him.

"You're always in a bad **mood** with me, Ralph," Mr. Green said. "Why? I don't—Here we go!"

A **pistol shot** had **signal**ed the start of the race. *Lovebug* and *Windswept* and the other racers **glide**d across the start line behind the motor-powered committee boat, which led them along a course **mark**ed by buoys with bright green **streamer**s.

Stanley **sat back**, enjoying himself. The sun was bright, the **breeze** fresh against his face, the sky clear and blue, the water a beautiful slate* color. There were boats

---

★ **slate** 점판암. 광물에 따라 초록색, 검은색 등을 띤다. 여기에서는 청회색을 나타내는 표현으로 쓰였다.

on both sides of them, boats ahead, boats behind. How pretty they were, their white sails making **cheerful crackling** sounds as they **billow**ed in the wind!

Along the **shore**, people waved from the **porch**es of houses, their voices carrying **faint**ly on the wind. "**Way to go**! . . . Looking good, **sailor**s! . . . Looking flat, one of them!" Stanley waved back, knowing that the **teasing** was kindly meant.

Lovebug passed other boats, but there were many more still ahead. And now they were almost **abreast** of *Windswept*.

Stanley saw that Jasper Green had **hoist**ed his spinnaker, and that other boats had too.

"I've got you beat, Ralph!" Jasper Green shouted.

"We'll just **round** this point, Stanley! Then—Now!" **exclaim**ed Ralph Jones. "Let's show Jasper what running before the wind really means!"

He **attach**ed his spinnaker to a halyard* and ran it up the **mast**. *Who-o-oosh!* The spinnaker billowed out, and Stanley felt

---

★ **halyard** 마룻줄. 항해할 때, 깃발이나 돛을 올리거나 내리기 위해 쓰는 밧줄.

Lovebug **surge** forward, as if pushed by an invisible hand.

"Here we go!" shouted Ralph Jones.

They passed five more boats, three more, then *Windswept!* They were ahead of everyone now, and the finish line lay ahead!

"We're going to win!" Stanley shouted.

"Yes!" Ralph Jones shouted back. "Just wait till Jasper—"

R-i-i-i-i-p!

The sound came from above. Looking up, they saw that the top of the spinnaker had **torn**.

R-i-i-i-i-i-i-p!

The rip **streak**ed **downward**, and now the spinnaker, torn all the way down,

flapped **useless**ly in the wind. *Lovebug*
slowed.

"Drat!*" Mr. Jones did his best with the
mainsail. "Drat, drat, drat!"

Windswept came up behind them. "**Tough
luck**!" called Jasper Green. "Ha, ha!"

"Drat!" Mr. Jones sighed. "Nothing
we can do, Stanley. Unless—This may be
crazy, but . . . Stanley, perhaps you could
be our spinnaker?"

"What?" Stanley shouted. "How?"

"Good question," said Mr. Jones. "Let's
see. . . . First, go **take hold of** the mast.
That's it. Now maybe—"

"Excuse me," Stanley said. "But did you

★ **drat** 제기랄! 젠장!

ever do this before?"

"Stanley, *nobody* ever did this before."
Mr. Jones took a deep breath. "Okay. Now
twist around to face forward, and **grab** the
mast behind you above your head!"

Stanley did as he was told, **plant**ing his
feet on the sides of the boat to hold him in
place. The wind **press**ed him from behind,
driving *Lovebug* toward the finish line.

"Yes! **Chest** forward! **Butt** back!"
shouted Mr. Jones. "Best spinnaker I
ever had!" In a moment they had passed
Windswept, and Stanley could not help
laughing at the surprise on Jasper Green's
face.

And then they were across the finish
line! *Lovebug* had won!

Back in the **clubhouse**, Jasper Green would not **admit** that he had lost. A flat person used as a sail? He had never seen *that* before, he said, and went to the race committee office to **complain**. But he returned shortly to **report** that *Lovebug* had indeed won. The committee had **advise**d him, he said, that there was no rule against a **crew** member allowing the wind to blow against him.

"Great sailing, Ralph!" he said. "I thought it was my race, I really did!"

"Thank you, Jasper," Mr. Jones said, but Stanley **notice**d that he did not smile.

Jasper Green noticed too. "Ralph, you're still mad at me," he said. "But *why?*"

"You **spill**ed coffee on my white pants,

Jasper," said Ralph Jones. "And you just laughed when I jumped up."

"What?" Jasper Green seemed greatly surprised. "I don't remember—Where? When?"

"We were having lunch," said Mr. Jones. "At the old Vandercook Hotel."

"The Vandercook? It **closed** **down** twenty years ago!" Mr. Green **slap**ped his **forehead**. "I *do* remember! That lunch was twenty years ago, Ralph!"

"Twenty-one, actually."

"All right, all right!" said Mr. Green. "I **apologize**, for heaven's **sake**!"

Ralph Jones smiled warmly. "Perfectly all right, Jasper," he said. "**Don't give it another thought.**"

Back to School

Stanley was **pleased** that his **classmate**s, who still remembered his **previous** flatness, made no great **fuss** about it now. Mostly they expressed only **cheerful** interest. "Feeling okay, Stan?" they said, and "Lookin' sharp, man! Sharp, see? Get the **joke**?" Only **mean** Emma Weeks was un**pleasant**. "Huh! Mr. **Show-off** again!"

Emma said one day, but Stanley pretended not to hear.

He had been back at school for a week when a newspaper, learning of this **unusual**ly shaped student, sent a photographer to **investigate**. He found Stanley watching a practice on the soccer **field**.

"Flash Tobin," he said. "From the *Daily Sentinel*. You're the flat kid, right?"

Stanley thought he must be joking. "How did you know?" he said, joking back.

"How did I—" The photographer laughed. "Oh, I get it! Can I take your picture, kid? Right here by the goal **post**s?"

Stanley **nod**ded, and Flash Tobin took his picture. "I heard there was a flat kid here before," he said. "Helped catch **sneak thieves** at the Famous Museum of Art.

But that kid, I heard he got round again."

"It was me," Stanley told him.

"You go **back and forth**, huh?" The photographer was **impress**ed. "Okay, get round now. I'd like a **shot** of that too."

"I can't just do it when I want," Stanley explained. "The first time, my brother had to blow me up. With a bicycle **pump**."

"Make a great picture!" Flash Tobin shook his head. "Well, we'll just go with flat."

Stanley's picture was in the *Daily Sentinel* the next morning, and Arthur could not help showing his **jealous**y. Stanley was always getting his picture in the paper, he said. Didn't they see how interesting it would be to have a picture of his brother?

There was a soccer team practice that afternoon, and the day was windy. It was **worrisome**, the **coach** said, the way

Stanley got blown about. Perhaps, for the **sake** of the team, he should **switch** to an **indoor** sport.

Stanley loved soccer, and the more he thought about what the coach had said, the sadder he felt.

Miss Elliott, his homeroom teacher,* **notice**d that he was not his usual cheerful self. "Mr. Redfield, the new **guidance counsel**or, is said to be very helpful to **trouble**d students," she told him. "I will ask him to find time for you."

Miss Elliott spoke to him again after lunch. "Such good luck, Stanley! Mr.

★ **homeroom teacher** 담임 선생님. 홈룸은 미국 학교에서 학생들이 출석 점호 등을 위해 모이는 교실을 말한다.

Redfield will see you right after school today!"

"Come in, Stanley. Sit right there!" Mr. Redfield pointed to a comfortable chair.

Stanley sat, and Mr. Redfield **lean**ed back behind his desk. "Now then. . . . You do understand that anything you say here is completely **confidential**? I won't tell anybody."

Stanley wondered what he could say that would interest anybody else.

"Miss Elliott tells me you seem troubled." Mr. Redfield **lower**ed his voice. "What's wrong?"

"I'm not sure, actually," Stanley said.

Mr. Redfield picked up a **pad** and a

pen. "Speak freely. Whatever comes into your head. Anything special happen lately?"

"Well, I got flat," Stanley said.

Mr. Redfield made a note on his pad. "I do see that, yes. How did that make you feel?"

Stanley thought for a moment. "Flat."

"I see." Mr. Redfield nodded. "This flatness, it's come upon you before, I'm told. Is it possible that somehow, without even **admit**ting it to yourself, you wanted it to happen again?"

"**No way!**" Stanley said **firm**ly. "The first time, it was kind of fun for a while. Flying like a **kite**, and being mailed to California, things like that. But then I got, you know, **tired** of it. And now I might get put off the soccer team."

Mr. Redfield nodded again. "You take no **pleasure** now in your unusual shape?"

Stanley thought for a moment. "Well, sometimes." He told about being a **sail**, and helping Ralph Jones win a **race**.

Mr. Redfield made another note. "I see. This dream of being a sail, have you dreamed it before?"

Stanley **stare**d at him. "It wasn't a . . . it really happened! I'm just tired of being different, I guess."

Mr. Redfield **press**ed his **fingertip**s together. "Different? How do you feel different, would you say?"

Stanley wondered how Mr. Redfield

could be a good guidance counselor if he had both **terrible eyesight** and a terrible memory.

"Well, I'm the only one in my class who's flat," he said. "The whole school, actually."

"Interesting." Mr. Redfield made another note and **glance**d at his watch. "I'm afraid our **time is up**, Stanley. Would you like to see me again? Just let Miss Elliott know."

"Okay," Stanley said politely, but he didn't think he would.

Why Me?

Stanley had looked sad all evening, Arthur thought. At **bedtime**, as they lay waiting for Mr. and Mrs. Lambchop to come say good night, he wondered how to **cheer** his brother up.

It was raining hard, and he remembered suddenly the rainy evening that Stanley had **snack**ed on raisins,* and by morning

had become in**visible**. A little-known
consequence, Dr. Dan had explained, of
eating fruit during bad weather.

"Hear the rain, Stanley?" he said. "Better
not eat any fruit."

"Ha, ha, ha." Stanley sounded **cross**.

———

★ **raisin** 건포도.

"Just leave me alone, okay?"

"Stanley's in a **terrible mood**," Arthur told Mr. and Mrs. Lambchop when they came in. "He won't even talk to me."

"What's wrong, my boy?" Mr Lambchop asked.

"Nothing." Stanley put his **pillow** over his head.

"If my picture was in the newspaper **practical**ly every day, I'd be happy," Arthur said. "I mean, why—"

Mrs. Lambchop **hush**ed him. "Stanley, **dear**? What is **troubling** you?"

"Nothing. Nothing," Stanley said from under the pillow, and sat up. "But why me? Why am I always getting flat, or invisible or something? Why can't it just once be someone else?"

"I wouldn't mind, actually," Arthur said. "Just for a while. I—"

"Hush, Arthur!" Mrs. Lambchop **put out** the **overhead** light, lit a corner lamp, and sat by Stanley on his bed. Mr. Lambchop sat with Arthur. The gentle **patter** of the rain against the windows, the **glow** of the little lamp, made the bedroom **cozy** indeed.

"I do see what you mean, Stanley," Mr. Lambchop said at last. "Why do these things happen to you? Your mother and I don't know the answer either. But things often happen without there seeming to be a reason, and then something else happens, and suddenly the first thing seems to have had a purpose **after all**."

"Well **put**, George!" Mrs. Lambchop **squeeze**d Stanley's hand. "What we do know, Stanley dear, is that we're very proud of you, and love you very much. And we understand about the flatness, and all the other un**expect**ed happenings, how **upset**ting it must be."

"It sure is!" said Stanley. "How would you like never knowing when you might get flat? Or invisible? Maybe someday I'll wake up ten feet* tall or one inch short, or with green hair, or a **tail** or something!"

"I know. . . ." Mrs. Lambchop said softly, and Mr. Lambchop came and **pat**ted

---

★ **feet** 길이의 단위 피트. 1피트는 약 30.48센티미터이다.

Stanley's shoulder. Then they kissed both boys, **switch**ed **off** the lamp, and went out.

Arthur spoke into the **darken**ed room. "Stanley?"

"I'm trying to sleep," said Stanley. "What?"

"I was just thinking," Arthur said. "If you got invisible, and then you got flat, how would they know?"

"Huh? I don't—" Stanley laughed. "Oh, I **get it**! About the flatness. Good one, Arthur."

Arthur laughed too.

"Quiet, please," said Stanley. "I'm trying to sleep."

"Okay," Arthur said, but he **chuckle**d several times before he fell asleep.

Emma

Mr. Lambchop came home early the next afternoon, full of excitement.

"Guess what?" he said. "The old Merker **Department Store downtown**? Eight floors, all **emptied** out, waiting to be **torn** down? Well, last night most of it fell down by itself!" He **switch**ed **on** the TV news. "Let's get the **latest**!"

"... more on the Merker building **collapse**!" a **newscaster** was saying. "It's just a mountain of **rubble** now, **folk**s! Three **workmen** have been **treat**ed for **minor bruise**s, but no other **injuries** are **report**ed. The public is **request**ed to **avoid** the area until—"

A young woman ran on, handed him a **slip** of paper, and ran off again.

"**Hold on**! This just in!" The newscaster read from the slip. "Wow! A little girl is **trap**ped under all that **wreckage**! Emma Weeks, daughter of **local businessman** Oswald Weeks!"

"Emma Weeks!" Stanley **exclaim**ed. "She's in my class! **No wonder** she wasn't at school today!"

"Emma's not hurt, it **appear**s," the newscaster continued. "**Firemen** called to the **scene** can hear her calling up through **chink**s in the wreckage, **demand**ing food and water! But Fire **Chief** Johnson has **forbid**den any **rescue effort**s! Any **disturb**ance, any **shift**ing of the wreckage,

he says, might bring the **rest**
of the building **crash**ing down!
Now, here's Tom Miller!"

The TV **screen** showed a **reporter**
with a microphone standing by
the **wreck**ed building.

"Emma Weeks!" shouted

the reporter, holding his microphone up
to a **crack**. "Do you hear me? Are you all
right?"

Emma's voice was **faint** but clear. "Oh,
sure! I'm just great! I hope a building falls
on me every day, you know? C'mon, get
me out of here!"

Mrs. Lambchop **sigh**ed. "Such an
unfortunate tone! She is under great
strain, of course."

"Emma's always like that," Stanley said.

Half an hour later, while Mrs.
Lambchop was preparing **supper**, a **siren**
sounded outside, then **died away**. Opening
the **front door**, Mr. Lambchop saw a
Fire **Department** car at the **curb**. On the
doorstep stood Fire Chief Johnson and a

very worried-looking man and woman.

"Mr. Lambchop?" said Chief Johnson. "I'll **get** right **to the point**, sir. I **reckon** you heard about little Emma Weeks, trapped in the Merker wreck? Well, Mr. and Mrs. Weeks here, and me, we'd like a word with you folks."

"Of course!" Mr. Lambchop led the visitors into the house and introduced them to his family.

"Oh, Mrs. Weeks!" Mrs. Lambchop cried. "Your poor daughter! You must be **dreadful**ly worried!"

"We are indeed!" said Mr. Weeks. "But Chief Johnson thinks your Stanley might be able to save Emma!"

"Who, me?" and "Who, Stanley?" said

Stanley and Arthur.

Chief Johnson explained. "Problem is that if a **policeman**, or one of my firemen, tries to **dig** his way in to Emma, the whole rest of the building could crash down on 'em! Too bad we don't have a flat fireman, I was thinking. Flat **fella** could **squeeze**

through all those **narrow opening**s we know are there, 'cause we hear Emma when she calls. Then I **recollect**ed the newspaper story, with a picture of Stanley here. **Hit** me right away! *That* boy could maybe **wiggle** in to Emma!"

For a moment, everyone was silent. Then Mrs. Lambchop shook her head.

"It sounds **terribly** dangerous," she said. "I'm sorry, but I must say no."

"It is a **tad risky**, ma'am," said Chief Johnson. "But we've got to remember the boy is already flat."

Mrs. Weeks **sob**bed. "Oh, poor Emma! How are we to save her?"

Mrs. Lambchop **bit** her **lip**.

Stanley remembered something. "I

was just thinking." He turned to Mr. Lambchop. "The other night? When I got mad about all the crazy things that keep happening to me? Remember what you said? You said that sometimes things happen that nobody can see a reason for, and then **afterwards** some other thing happens, and **all of a sudden** it seems like the first thing had a reason **after all**. Well, I was just thinking that me getting flat again was one crazy thing, and that maybe Emma getting **stuck** where I'm the only one who can try to save her, that might be the second thing."

Mr. Lambchop **nod**ded, and took Mrs. Lambchop's hand. "We should be very proud of our son, Harriet."

Mrs. Lambchop thought for a moment. "Stanley," she said at last. "Will you be very, very, careful not to let that **enormous** building fall on you?"

"Okay. Sure," Stanley said.

Mrs. Lambchop turned to Mr. and Mrs. Weeks. "We will allow Stanley to help," she said. "He will do his best for Emma."

"Fine boy we got here! Brave as a lion!" shouted Chief Johnson. "Now listen up, folks! Mrs. Lambchop, you help me get things ready! Then Stanley can go right in after Emma! Got that? Everybody meet us at the Merker Building, thirty minutes from now!"

Where Are You, Emma?

In the late afternoon sunlight, at the **remain**s of the old Merker building, the Lambchops and the Weekses watched **Chief** Johnson prepare Stanley for his **rescue attempt**. Flash Tobin, the *Daily Sentinel* photographer, was there too, taking pictures.

Mrs. Lambchop had **supplied** two **slices**

of bread and cheese, each **wrap**ped in
plastic,* and her grandfather's flat silver
cigarette case filled with grape soda.*
Chief Johnson **tape**d the bread and cheese
packets to Stanley's arms and legs, the
cigarette case to his **chest**, and gave him a
small, flat **flashlight**.

Then he led Stanley up to a tall **crack**
in the **wreckage**. "Emma!" he shouted.
"**Fella**'s coming to help you! When he calls
your name, you **holler** back 'Here!' so he
knows which way to go. Got that?"

Emma's voice came **faint**ly. "Yeah, yeah!
Hurry up! I'm **starving**!"

★ **plastic** 여기에서는 비닐봉투를 말한다.
✽ **soda** 탄산음료. 이산화탄소를 물에 녹여 만든, 맛이 산뜻하고 시원한 음
료.

Chief Johnson shook Stanley's hand. "Get going, son!"

The evening sunlight **glow**ed warmly on the red **brick**s of the fallen building as Stanley stepped close to the crack. Mrs. Lambchop **wave**d to him, and Stanley waved back. How handsome he is, she thought. How brave, how tall, how flat!

Stanley took two steps forward and **disappear**ed **sideways** through the crack. A moment later they heard his shout. "Hey! It's really dark in here!"

"**Hay** is for horses, Stanley!" Mrs. Lambchop called back. "Oh, **never mind**! Good luck, **dear**!"

This was a dark greater than any he had

ever known. Stanley could almost feel the blackness on his skin. He **click**ed on his flashlight and **edge**d forward without **difficulty**, but then the crack **narrow**ed, slowing him. The bread slice on his left leg had **scrape**d something, **loosen**ing the tape that held it. **Press**ing the tape back into place, he **wiggle**d forward until he came to what seemed a **dead end**, but a little **swing** of the flashlight showed cracks **branch**ing right and left.

"Emma?" he called.

"Here!"

Her voice came from the right, so he moved along that branch. "Emma?"

"Yeah, yeah! What?"

"When I say your name, you're

supposed to say 'Here!'"

"I already did that!"

He followed another crack to the left. "Emma?"

There was no answer. Stanley managed a few more feet and then, quite suddenly, the crack **widen**ed. He called again. "Emma?"

"Bananas!"

"Keep talking," he shouted. "I need to hear you!"

"Bananas! Here! **Blah**, blah! Whatever! Hey, I can see your light!"

And there she was. The crack had widened to become a small **cave**, at the back of which sat Emma. Her jeans and shirt were **smudge**d with **dirt**, but it was most surely Emma, **squint**ing against the brightness of his light.

"You!" she **exclaim**ed. "From school! The flattie!"

Don't lose your **temper**, Stanley told himself. "I was the only one they thought could get in here. How are you doing, Emma?"

Emma **roll**ed **her eyes**. "Oh, just great! A whole building falls on me, and they send in a flattie! And now I'm starving to death!"

Stanley untaped the slices of bread and cheese, and handed them over.

"Cheese, huh?" Emma put her sandwich together and took a **bite**. "I hate cheese. Got anything to drink, flattie?"

"Please don't call me flattie. Here." He held out the silver cigarette case.

Emma rolled her eyes again. "I'm not allowed to smoke."

"It's soda."

She opened the cigarette case and **sip**ped. "Blaahh! I hate grape!"

Chief Johnson's voice rose from a hole

in the wall behind her. "Stanley? You there
yet?"

Emma **jerk**ed a **thumb** at the hole. "It's
for you, flattie."

"I'm here, Chief!" Stanley called.
"Emma's okay."

He heard **cheer**ing, and then the Chief's
voice came again. "See a way out, Stan?"

"I haven't had a chance to look around
yet. Emma's eating."

"We'll wait. Over and out, Stan!"

"You too!" Stanley called.

He waited until Emma had finished her
sandwich. "Emma, how did you get into
this **mess**? What made you come in here?"

"I just came over to look," Emma said.
"And they had all these **sign**s! 'Danger!

Keep out!' All over the place, even behind in the **parking lot**. 'Keep out! Danger! Danger!' I really hate that, you know? So there was this door, and it was open, so I went in." She finished the grape soda. "Okay, let's go."

"Not the way I came in," Stanley said. "I could just **barely squeeze** through. And we have to be careful, because—"

"I know!" Emma **interrupt**ed. "Chief whatshisname kept telling me: 'Don't move around! The whole **rest** of the building might **crash** down!' So am I supposed to live down here forever?"

"This door you came through," Stanley said. "How far did you come to find this sort of cave we're in?"

"Who said anything about far? I just got inside, and there were these crashing noises, and the whole building was shaking, and I fell down right here! The crashing **went on** forever! I thought I was going to die!"

"Calm down." An idea came into Stanley's head. "Just where was this door? Do you remember?"

"Over there somewhere." Emma pointed into the darkness of a corner behind her.

Stanley swung his light, but saw only what seemed to be a **solid** wall of **splinter**ed **board**s, rock, and brick.

Emma pointed a **bit** left, then right. "Maybe there . . . I don't know! Was I

supposed to take pictures or something?
What difference does it make?"

"We might be just a little bit inside that
door," Stanley said. "And what we want is
to be just outside of it."

Moving closer to the corner, he saw that
a **jagged** piece of wood **protrude**d at **waist**
level. It came out easily when he **tug**ged,
followed by **loose** dirt.

Emma stood beside him. "Why are you
making this mess?"

He **poke**d in the hole with the **stick**.
"Maybe I'll find—"

Dirt **cascade**d from the wall, **cover**ing
his shoes. He saw light now, not just
the little circle from his flashlight, but
daylight! Unmistakably daylight!

"Oooohhhh!" said Emma.

Stanley made the hole still larger, and they saw that a door lay on its side across the **bottom** of the hole, wreckage **limit**ing the **opening** on both sides. But it was big enough! They would be able to wiggle through! He ran back to the wall from which Chief Johnson's voice had come.

"We're on our way out!" he shouted. "We'll be in back, in the **courtyard**!"

"**Got it**!" came the Chief's voice. "Great work!"

Stanley turned to Emma. "Let's go!"

"I'll get all dirty," Emma said. "Maybe we could just—"

"Come ON!"

"Don't **yell**!" Emma said, but she **crawl**ed quickly through the hole with Stanley right behind her.

Hero!

There was much **rejoicing** in the
courtyard. Mrs. Lambchop kissed Stanley
and Arthur. Mrs. Weeks kissed Emma,
and then everyone else, even Flash Tobin,
who had arrived to take pictures. Mr.
Lambchop shook hands with Mr. Weeks
and **Chief** Johnson, who **announce**d
several times that Stanley was a great

hero.

Flash Tobin took a group picture of all the Lambchops. "Need one more," he said. "Emma, just you and Stanley. Your hero, right? Saved your life!"

"I could have got out by myself," Emma said. "I just didn't know **exact**ly where the door was." But she went to stand by Stanley.

"Smile!" Flash Tobin took the picture. "Yes, that's good!" He gave Stanley a **cheerful slap** on the back, just as Emma's **elbow jab**bed hard into Stanley's **rib**s.

"Owww!" Stanley **yell**ed.

Emma **grin**ned. "That's for you, Mr. Hero!"

"Are you crazy? What—" Stanley

stopped. Everybody was **staring** at him.

He felt **peculiar**, as if—Yes! He was getting

round again!

"Wow!" Emma said. "How do you do

that?"

"**Hooray** for you, dear!" shouted Mrs. Lambchop, and more cries rose from the others in the courtyard. "Do you see what I see? . . . He's blowing up! . . . Are we crazy or what?"

Flash Tobin **aim**ed his camera again. "**Hold it**, kid!"

But he was too late. Before him now stood a smiling Stanley Lambchop, shaped like a **regular** boy!

Mr. Lambchop ran to hug him, and everyone else **applaud**ed.

"Been thirty years with the Fire **Department**, and never saw anything like that!" said Chief Johnson. "Wouldn't have missed it!"

"I'm really glad," Stanley said. "But what made it happen?"

"What Dr. Dan said!" shouted Arthur. "Remember? The Osteo-posteo-whatever!"

"The OBP! The **Osteal** Balance Point." Mr. Lambchop smiled. "Yes! The slap on the back from Flash Tobin, and the **poke** from Emma! That did it!"

A **board** fell from the **tilt**ing **roof** of the Merker Building, **land**ing in a corner of the courtyard.

"Let's go, **folk**s," said Chief Johnson. "We're not safe here!"

A moment later, back out in the street, there was more hugging and kissing and saying good night. Suddenly, behind them, there were great **creak**ing and **grind**ing sounds. Turning, they watched what was left of the Merker building come **crash**ing down.

Emma spoke first. "Oh, boy," she said softly. "Wow!"

Mrs. Weeks **caught her eye**, and gave a little **nod** toward Stanley.

Emma looked **puzzle**d. "Huh? . . . Oh, yeah!" She turned to Stanley. "I guess maybe you, you know, saved my life. Whatever." She kissed his **cheek**. "Thank you very much, Stanley Lambchop."

"It's okay," Stanley said, quite red in the face. "You're welcome."

Everyone went home.

Fame!

At **bedtime** the next evening, the
Lambchops read again the *Daily Sentinel*
they had enjoyed so much at breakfast that
morning.

The front page **headline** read: RUDE
GIRL SAVED! FLAT **RESCUER REGAINS** SHAPE!
Beneath that were two Flash Tobin
photographs—the Lambchop family

THE DAILY S
RUDE GIRL SAVE
FLAT RESCUER
REGAINS SHAPE!

picture and the one of Stanley and Emma taken just before she **poke**d him in the **rib**s. Arthur was **particular**ly **pleased** with the family picture.

"Finally!" he said. "Not just Stanley! People could have been wondering if he had a brother, you know? Can I have this one?"

"You may," said Mrs. Lambchop. "I want the one of Stanley with Emma, for my kitchen wall."

"I don't care about pictures," Stanley said. "I just hope I never go back to being flat."

Mrs. Lambchop **pat**ted his hand. "I told Dr. Dan of your **recover**y, **dear**. He thinks it most **unlikely** the flatness will **occur** again."

"Yay!" said Stanley.

Arthur cut the family picture out of the paper, and used a red pencil to draw an **arrow**, pointing up at him, in the white space at the **bottom**. Under the arrow, he wrote, *Hero's Brother.* Then he **tape**d the picture to the wall above his bed.

Soon all the Lambchops were asleep.

The End

HERO'S BROTHER

스탠리, 다시 납작해지다!

스탠리, 다시 납작해지다!

CONTENTS

미국 초등학생 사이에서 저스틴 비버보다 더 유명한 소년, 플랫 스탠리!

『플랫 스탠리(Flat Stanley)』 시리즈는 미국의 작가 제프 브라운(Jeff Brown)이 쓴 책으로, 한밤중에 몸 위로 떨어진 거대한 게시판에 눌려 납작해진(flat) 스탠리 가 겪는 다양한 모험을 담고 있습니다. 플랫 스탠리는 아동 도서이지만 부모님 들과 선생님들에게도 큰 사랑을 받으며, 출간된 지 50년이 넘은 지금까지 여러 세대를 아우르며 독자들에게 재미를 주고 있습니다. 미국에서만 100만 부 이상 판매된 『플랫 스탠리』 시리즈는 기존 챕터북 시리즈와 함께 플랫 스탠리의 세계 모험(Flat Stanley's Worldwide Adventures) 시리즈, 리더스북 등 다양한 형태로 출판되었고, 여러 언어로 번역되어 전 세계 독자들의 마음을 사로잡았습니다. 주인공 스탠리가 그려진 종이 인형을 만들어 이를 우편으로 원하는 사람에게 보 내는 플랫 스탠리 프로젝트(The Flat Stanley Project)가 1995년에 시작된 이후, 이 책은 더 많은 관심을 받게 되었습니다. 유명 연예인은 물론 오바마 대통령까 지 이 종이 인형과 함께 사진을 찍어 공유하는 등, 수많은 사례를 통해 시리즈의 높은 인기를 짐작할 수 있습니다.
이러한 『플랫 스탠리』 시리즈는 한국에서도 널리 알려져 '엄마표·아빠표 영어' 를 진행하는 부모님과 초보 영어 학습자라면 반드시 읽어야 하는 영어원서로 자 리 잡았습니다. 렉사일 지수가 최대 640L인 플랫 스탠리는 간결하지만 필수적 인 어휘로 쓰여, 영어원서가 친숙하지 않은 학습자들에게도 즐거운 원서 읽기 경험을 선사할 것입니다.

번역과 단어장이 포함된 워크북, 그리고 오디오북까지 담긴 풀 패키지!

이 책은 영어원서 『플랫 스탠리』 시리즈에, 탁월한 학습 효과를 거둘 수 있도록 다양한 콘텐츠를 덧붙인 책입니다.

- **영어원서:** 본문에 나온 어려운 어휘에 볼드 처리가 되어 있어 단어를 더욱 분 명하게 인지할 수 있고, 문맥에 따른 자연스러운 암기 효과를 얻을 수 있습니다.
- **단어장:** 원서에 볼드 처리된 어휘의 의미가 완벽하게 정리되어 있어 사전 없 이 원서를 수월하게 읽을 수 있으며, 반복해서 등장하는 단어에 '복습' 표기를 하여 자연스럽게 복습을 돕도록 구성했습니다.

- **번역:** 영문과 비교할 수 있도록 직역에 가까운 번역을 담았습니다. 원서 읽기에 익숙하지 않은 초보 학습자도 어려움 없이 내용을 파악할 수 있습니다.
- **퀴즈:** 챕터별로 내용을 확인하는 이해력 점검 퀴즈가 들어 있습니다.
- **오디오북:** 미국 현지에서 판매 중인 빠른 속도의 오디오북(분당 약 145단어)과 국내에서 녹음된 따라 읽기용 오디오북(분당 약 110단어)을 기본으로 포함하고 있어, 듣기 훈련은 물론 소리 내어 읽기에까지 폭넓게 활용할 수 있습니다.

이 책의 수준과 타깃 독자

- 미국 원어민 기준: 유치원 ~ 초등학교 저학년
- 한국 학습자 기준: 초등학교 저학년 ~ 중학생
- 영어원서 완독 경험이 없는 초보 영어 학습자
- 도서 분량: 약 5,900단어
- 비슷한 수준의 다른 챕터북: Arthur Chapter Book,★ The Zack Files,★ Tales from the Odyssey,★ Junie B. Jones,★ Magic Tree House, Marvin Redpost

  ★ 「롱테일 에디션」으로 출간된 도서

『플랫 스탠리』 이렇게 읽어 보세요!

- **단어 암기는 이렇게!** 처음 리딩을 시작하기 전, 오늘 읽을 챕터에 나오는 단어들을 눈으로 쭉 훑어봅니다. 모르는 단어는 좀 더 주의 깊게 보되, 손으로 쓰면서 완벽하게 암기할 필요는 없습니다. 본문을 읽으면서 이 단어를 다시 만나게 되는데, 그 과정에서 단어의 쓰임새와 어감을 자연스럽게 익히게 됩니다. 이렇게 책을 읽은 후에 단어를 다시 한번 복습하세요. 복습할 때는 중요하다고 생각하는 단어들을 손으로 쓰면서 꼼꼼하게 외우는 것도 좋습니다. 이런 방식으로 책을 읽으면 많은 단어를 빠르고 부담 없이 익힐 수 있습니다.

- **리딩할 때는 리딩에만 집중하자!** 원서를 읽는 중간중간 모르는 단어가 나온다고 워크북을 바로 펼쳐 보거나, 곧바로 번역을 찾아보는 것은 크게 도움이 되지 않습니다. 모르는 단어나 이해되지 않는 문장들은 따로 가볍게 표시만 해 두고, 전체적인 맥락을 파악하며 속도감 있게 읽어 나가세요. 리딩을 할 때는 속

도에 대한 긴장감을 잃지 않으면서 리딩에만 집중하는 것이 좋습니다. 모르는 단어와 문장은 리딩을 마친 후에 한꺼번에 정리하는 '리뷰' 시간을 통해 점검하는 시간을 가지면 됩니다. 리뷰를 할 때는 번역은 물론 단어장과 사전도 꼼꼼하게 확인하면서 어떤 이유에서 이해가 되지 않았는지 생각해 봅니다.

- **번역 활용은 이렇게!** 이해가 가지 않는 문장은 번역을 통해서 그 의미를 파악할 수 있습니다. 하지만 한국어와 영어는 정확히 1:1 대응이 되지 않기 때문에 번역을 활용하는 데에도 지혜가 필요합니다. 의역이 된 부분까지 억지로 의미를 대응해서 이해하려고 하기보다, 어떻게 그런 의미가 만들어진 것인지 추측하면서 번역은 참고 자료로 활용하는 것이 좋습니다.

- **듣기 훈련은 이렇게!** 리스닝 실력을 향상시키고 싶다면 오디오북을 적극적으로 활용해 보세요. 처음에는 오디오북을 틀어 놓고 눈으로 해당 내용을 따라 읽으면서 훈련을 하고, 이것이 익숙해지면 오디오북만 틀어 놓고 '귀를 통해' 책을 읽어 보세요. 눈으로 읽지 않은 책이라도 귀를 통해 이해할 수 있을 정도가 되면, 이후에 영어 듣기로 어려움을 겪는 일은 거의 없을 것입니다.

- **소리 내어 읽고 녹음하자!** 이 책은 특히 소리 내어 읽기(voice reading)에 최적화된 문장 길이와 구조를 가지고 있습니다. 오디오북 기본 구성에 포함된 '따라 읽기용' 오디오북을 활용해 소리 내어 읽기 훈련을 시작해 보세요! 내가 읽은 것을 녹음하고 들어보는 과정을 통해 자연스럽게 어휘와 표현을 복습하고, 의식적·무의식적으로 발음을 교정하게 됩니다. 이렇게 영어로 소리를 만들어 본 경험은 이후 탄탄한 스피킹 실력의 밑거름이 될 것입니다.

- **2~3번 반복해서 읽자!** 영어 초보자라면 처음부터 완벽하게 이해하려고 하는 것보다는 2~3회 반복해서 읽을 것을 추천합니다. 처음 원서를 읽을 때는 생소한 단어들과 스토리 때문에 내용 파악에 급급할 수밖에 없습니다. 하지만 일단 내용을 파악한 후에 다시 읽으면 문장 구조나 어휘의 활용에 더 집중하게 되고, 원서를 더 깊이 있게 읽을 수 있습니다. 그 과정에서 리딩 속도에 탄력이 붙고 리딩 실력 또한 더 확고히 다지게 됩니다.

- **'시리즈'로 꾸준히 읽자!** 한 작가의 책을 시리즈로 읽는 것 또한 영어 실력 향상에 큰 도움이 됩니다. 같은 등장인물이 다시 나오기 때문에 내용 파악이 더 수월할 뿐 아니라, 작가가 사용하는 어휘와 표현들도 반복되기 때문에 탁월한 복습 효과까지 얻을 수 있습니다. 롱테일북스의 『플랫 스탠리』 시리즈는 현재 6권, 총 35,700단어 분량이 출간되어 있습니다. 시리즈를 꾸준히 읽다 보면 영어 실력이 자연스럽게 향상될 것입니다.

원서 본문 구성

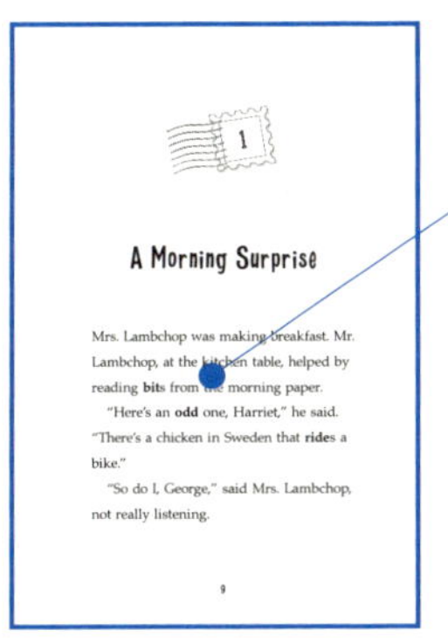

<u>내용이 담긴 원서 본문입니다.</u>
원어민이 읽는 일반 원서와 같은 텍스트지만, 암기해야 할 중요 어휘들은 볼드체로 표시되어 있습니다. 이 어휘들은 지금 들고 계신 워크북에 챕터별로 정리되어 있습니다.

학습 심리학 연구 결과에 따르면, 한 단어씩 따로 외우는 단어 암기는 거의 효과가 없다고 합니다. 단어를 제대로 외우기 위해서는 문맥(context) 속에서 단어를 암기해야 하며, 한 단어당 문맥 속에서 15번 이상 마주칠 때 완벽하게 암기할 수 있다고 합니다.

이 책의 본문에서는 중요 어휘를 볼드체로 강조하여, 문맥 속의 단어들을 더 확실히 인지(word cognition in context)하도록 돕고 있습니다. 또한 대부분의 중요 단어들은 다른 챕터에서도 반복해서 등장하기 때문에 이 책을 읽는 것만으로도 자연스럽게 어휘력을 향상시킬 수 있습니다.

본문 하단에는 내용 이해를 돕기 위한 <u>'각주'가 첨가되어 있습니다.</u> 각주는 굳이 암기할 필요는 없지만, 알아 두면 도움이 될 만한 정보를 설명하고 있습니다. 각주를 참고하면 스토리를 더 깊이 있게 이해할 수 있어 원서를 읽는 재미가 배가됩니다.

"Listen to this. 'Merker Building **emptied**. To be **collapsed** next week.' **Imagine**! Eight floors!"
"Poor thing!" Mrs. Lambchop **set out plates**. "Boys!" she called. "Breakfast is ready!"
Her **glance** fell upon a **row** of photographs on the wall above the **sink**. There was a smiling Stanley, only half an inch* thick, his big **bulletin board** having fallen from the bedroom wall to **rest** upon him **overnight**. Next came **reminders** of the many family **adventures** that had come after Stanley's younger brother, Arthur, had **cleverly** blown him round

* inch 길이의 단위 인치. 1인치는 약 2.54센티미터이다

워크북(Workbook) 구성

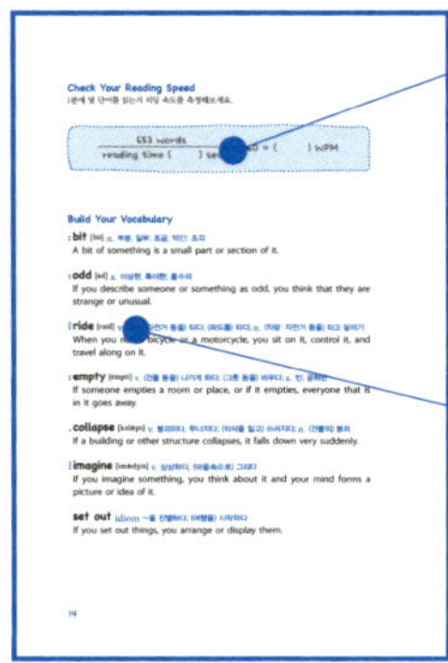

Check Your Reading Speed
해당 챕터의 단어 수가 기록되어 있어, 리딩 속도를 측정할 수 있습니다. 특히 리딩 속도를 중시하는 독자들이 유용하게 사용할 수 있습니다.

Build Your Vocabulary
본문에 볼드 표시되어 있는 단어들이 정리되어 있습니다. 리딩 전·후에 반복해서 보면 원서를 더욱 쉽게 읽을 수 있고, 어휘력도 빠르게 향상될 것입니다.

단어는 〈스펠링 – 빈도 – 발음기호 – 품사 – 한글 뜻 – 영문 뜻〉 순서로 표기되어 있으며 빈도 표시(★)가 많을수록 필수 어휘입니다. 반복해서 등장하는 단어는 빈도 대신 '복습'으로 표기되어 있습니다. 품사는 아래와 같이 표기했습니다.

n. 명사 | **a.** 형용사 | **ad.** 부사 | **v.** 동사

conj. 접속사 | **prep.** 전치사 | **int.** 감탄사 | **idiom** 숙어 및 관용구

Comprehension Quiz
간단한 퀴즈를 통해 읽은 내용에 대한 이해력을 점검해 볼 수 있습니다.

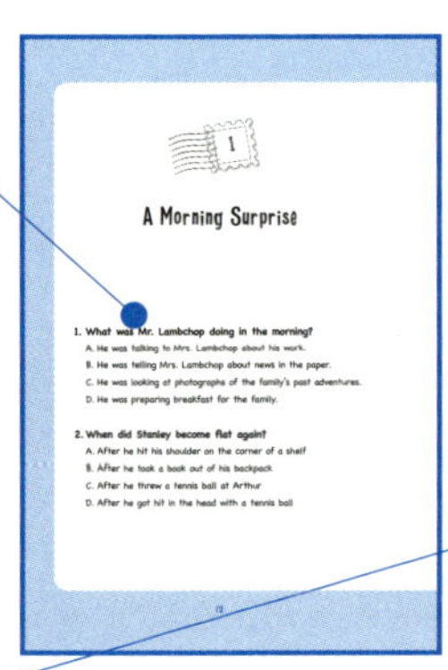

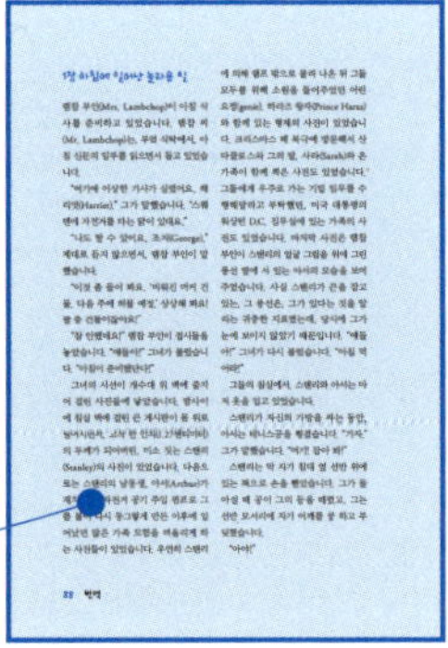

한국어 번역
영문과 비교할 수 있도록 최대한 직역에 가까운 번역을 담았습니다.

오디오북 구성

이 책에는 '듣기 훈련'과 '소리 내어 읽기 훈련'을 위한 2가지 종류의 오디오북이
기본으로 포함되어 있습니다.

- **듣기 훈련용 오디오북:** 분당 145단어 속도 (미국 현지에서 판매 중인 오디오북)
- **따라 읽기용 오디오북:** 분당 110단어 속도 (소리 내어 읽기 훈련용 오디오북)

QR코드를 인식하여 따라 읽기용 & 듣기 훈련용 두 가지 오디오북을 들어
보세요! 더불어 롱테일북스 홈페이지 (www.longtailbooks.co.kr)에서도
오디오북 MP3 파일을 다운로드 받을 수 있습니다.

A Morning Surprise

1. What was Mr. Lambchop doing in the morning?

    A. He was talking to Mrs. Lambchop about his work.

    B. He was telling Mrs. Lambchop about news in the paper.

    C. He was looking at photographs of the family's past adventures.

    D. He was preparing breakfast for the family.

2. When did Stanley become flat again?

    A. After he hit his shoulder on the corner of a shelf

    B. After he took a book out of his backpack

    C. After he threw a tennis ball at Arthur

    D. After he got hit in the head with a tennis ball

3. **What did Arthur do to try to help Stanley?**
    A. He used a bicycle pump to try to get air into Stanley.
    B. He had Stanley lie down so that he wouldn't feel any pain.
    C. He told Stanley to stay still so that he wouldn't get even
       flatter.
    D. He put a hose in Stanley's mouth to try to pump air out of
       him.

4. **What favor did Stanley ask of Arthur?**
    A. He asked Arthur to hide him from Mr. and Mrs. Lambchop.
    B. He asked Arthur to lie to Mr. and Mrs. Lambchop.
    C. He asked Arthur to distract Mr. and Mrs. Lambchop.
    D. He asked Arthur to tell Mr. and Mrs. Lambchop what had
       happened.

5. **How did Mr. Lambchop react when he saw Stanley was
   flat again?**
    A. He didn't think Stanley should go to school.
    B. He was worried about whether Stanley was hurt.
    C. He felt Stanley being flat again was a good thing.
    D. He thought the bulletin board had fallen on top of Stanley
       again.

Check Your Reading Speed

1분에 몇 단어를 읽는지 리딩 속도를 측정해보세요.

$$\frac{653 \text{ words}}{\text{reading time (\quad) sec}} \times 60 = (\quad\quad) \text{ WPM}$$

Build Your Vocabulary

☆ **bit** [bit] n. 부분, 일부; 조금, 약간; 조각
A bit of something is a small part or section of it.

☆ **odd** [ad] a. 이상한, 특이한; 홀수의
If you describe someone or something as odd, you think that they are strange or unusual.

☆ **empty** [émpti] v. (건물 등을) 나가게 하다; (그릇 등을) 비우다; a. 빈; 공허한
If someone empties a room or place, or if it empties, everyone that is in it goes away.

⋆ **collapse** [kəlǽps] v. 붕괴되다, 무너지다; (의식을 잃고) 쓰러지다; n. (건물의) 붕괴
If a building or other structure collapses, it falls down very suddenly.

☆ **imagine** [imǽdʒin] v. 상상하다, (마음속으로) 그리다
If you imagine something, you think about it and your mind forms a picture or idea of it.

set out idiom ~을 진열하다; (여행을) 시작하다
If you set out things, you arrange or display them.

☆ **plate** [pleit] n. 접시, 그릇; 판; (자동차) 번호판
A plate is a round or oval flat dish that is used to hold food.

⋆ **glance** [glæns] n. 흘낏 봄; v. 흘낏 보다; 대충 훑어보다
A glance is a quick look at someone or something.

14

row [rou] n. 열, 줄; 노 젓기; v. 노를 젓다
A row of things or people is a number of them arranged in a line.

sink [siŋk] n. (부엌의) 개수대; v. 가라앉다, 빠지다; (구멍을) 파다
A sink is a large fixed container in a kitchen, with taps to supply water.
It is mainly used for washing dishes.

bulletin board [búlitən bɔ:rd] n. 게시판
A bulletin board is a board which is usually attached to a wall in order
to display notices giving information about something.

rest [rest] v. 놓이다, (~에) 있다; 쉬다; n. 휴식; 나머지
If something is resting somewhere, or if you are resting it there, it is in
a position where its weight is supported.

overnight [òuvərnáit] ad. 밤사이에, 하룻밤 동안
If something happens overnight, it happens throughout the night or at
some point during the night.

remind [rimáind] v. 상기시키다, 다시 한 번 알려 주다 (reminder n. 생각나게 하는 것)
Something that serves as a reminder of another thing makes you think
about the other thing.

adventure [ædvénʧər] n. 모험; 모험심
If someone has an adventure, they become involved in an unusual,
exciting, and rather dangerous journey or series of events.

clever [klévər] a. 기발한, 재치 있는; 영리한, 똑똑한 (cleverly ad. 솜씨 좋게)
A clever idea, book, or invention is extremely effective and shows the
skill of the people involved.

pump [pʌmp] n. 펌프; 펌프 사용; v. (펌프로) 퍼 올리다; (거세게) 솟구치다
(bicycle pump n. 자전거 공기 주입 펌프)
A pump is a machine or device that is used to force a liquid or gas to
flow in a particular direction.

grant [grænt] v. 승인하다, 허락하다; 인정하다; n. 보조금
If someone in authority grants you something, or if something is granted
to you, you are allowed to have it.

★ **accidental** [æksədéntl] a. 우연한, 돌발적인 (accidentally ad. 우연히, 뜻하지 않게)
An accidental event happens by chance or as the result of an accident, and is not deliberately intended.

★ **summon** [sʌ́mən] v. 호출하다, (오라고) 부르다; 소환하다
If you summon someone, you order them to come to you.

☆ **pole** [poul] n. (지구의) 극; 막대기, 기둥 (North Pole n. 북극)
The North Pole is the place on the surface of the earth which is farthest toward the north.

☆ **president** [prézədənt] n. 대통령; 회장
The president of a country that has no king or queen is the person who is the head of state of that country.

☆ **undertake** [ʌ̀ndərtéik] v. 착수하다; 약속하다
When you undertake a task or job, you start doing it and accept responsibility for it.

★ **mission** [míʃən] n. 임무; 우주 비행
A mission is an important task that people are given to do, especially one that involves traveling to another country.

outer space [autər spéis] n. (대기권 외) 우주 공간
Outer space is the area outside the earth's atmosphere where the other planets and stars are situated.

☆ **string** [striŋ] n. 끈, 줄; 일련; v. 묶다, 매달다; (실 등에) 꿰다
String is thin rope made of twisted threads, used for tying things together or tying up parcels.

☆ **valuable** [vǽljuəbl] a. 소중한, 귀중한; 값비싼
If you describe something or someone as valuable, you mean that they are very useful and helpful.

★ **presence** [prezns] n. (특정한 곳에) 있음, 존재(함), 참석
Someone's presence in a place is the fact that they are there.

visible [vízəbl] a. (눈에) 보이는, 알아볼 수 있는; 뚜렷한 (invisible a. 보이지 않는)
If you describe something as invisible, you mean that it cannot be seen, for example because it is transparent, hidden, or very small.

dress [dres] v. 옷을 입다; n. 드레스; 옷 (dressing n. 옷 입기)
When you dress or dress yourself, you put on clothes.

backpack [bǽkpæk] n. 배낭
A backpack is a bag with straps that go over your shoulders, so that you can carry things on your back when you are walking or climbing.

bounce [bauns] v. (공 등이) 튀다, 뛰어오르다; 깡충깡충 뛰다; n. (공 등이) 튐; 탄력
When an object such as a ball bounces or when you bounce it, it moves upward from a surface or away from it immediately after hitting it.

reach [riːʃ] v. (손·팔을) 뻗다; ~에 이르다; n. (닿을 수 있는) 거리; 범위
If you reach somewhere, you move your arm and hand to take or touch something.

shelf [ʃelf] n. 선반; (책장의) 칸
A shelf is a flat piece of wood, metal, or glass which is attached to a wall or to the sides of a cupboard.

strike [straik] v. (struck–struck/stricken) (세게) 치다, 부딪치다; (갑자기) 공격하다; n. 공격; 치기, 때리기
If you strike someone or something, you deliberately hit them.

bang [bæŋ] v. 쿵 하고 찧다; 쾅 하고 치다; 쾅 하고 닫다; n. 쾅 (하는 소리)
If you bang a part of your body, you accidentally knock it against something and hurt yourself.

ouch [auʧ] int. 아야!
'Ouch!' is used in writing to represent the noise that people make when they suddenly feel pain.

adjust [ədʒʌ́st] v. (매무새 등을) 바로잡다; 조정하다; 적응하다
If you adjust something such as your clothing or a machine, you correct or alter its position or setting.

✿ **pause** [pɔːz] v. (말·일을 하다가) 잠시 멈추다; n. (말·행동 등의) 멈춤
If you pause while you are doing something, you stop for a short period
and then continue.

✿ **swallow** [swálou] v. 마른침을 삼키다; (음식 등을) 삼키다; n. [동물] 제비
If you swallow, you make a movement in your throat as if you are
swallowing something, often because you are nervous or frightened.

★ **stare** [stɛər] v. 빤히 쳐다보다, 응시하다; n. 빤히 쳐다보기, 응시
If you stare at someone or something, you look at them for a long time.

✿ **fetch** [fetʃ] v. 가지고 오다, 데리고 오다; (특정 가격에) 팔리다; n. 가져옴, 데려옴
If you fetch something or someone, you go and get them from the place
where they are.

✿ **chest** [tʃest] ① n. 상자, 궤 ② n. 가슴, 흉부
A chest is a large, heavy box used for storing things.

★ **hose** [houz] n. 호스; v. 호스로 물을 뿌리다
A hose is a long, flexible pipe made of rubber or plastic, which is used
to direct water onto fires or gardens.

✿ **steady** [stédi] a. 꾸준한; 흔들림 없는, 안정된; v. 흔들리지 않다; 진정되다
A steady situation continues or develops gradually without any
interruptions and is not likely to change quickly.

make a face idiom 얼굴을 찌푸리다, 침울한 표정을 짓다
If you make a face, you twist your face to indicate a certain mental or
emotional state.

★ **snatch** [snætʃ] v. 와락 붙잡다, 잡아채다; 간신히 얻다; n. 잡아 뺏음, 강탈
If you snatch something or snatch at something, you take it or pull it
away quickly.

✿ **favor** [féivər] n. 호의; 지지, 인정; v. 선호하다; 알맞다
If you do someone a favor, you do something for them even though
you do not have to.

★ **doorway** [dɔ́ːrwèi] n. 출입구
A doorway is a space in a wall where a door opens and closes.

★ **hay** [hei] n. 건초
Hay is grass which has been cut and dried so that it can be used to
feed animals.

‡ **dear** [diər] n. 얘야; 여보, 당신; int. 이런!; 맙소사!; a. 사랑하는; ~에게
You can call someone dear as a sign of affection.

★ **sigh** [sai] v. 한숨을 쉬다, 한숨짓다; 탄식하듯 말하다; n. 한숨
When you sigh, you let out a deep breath, as a way of expressing feelings
such as disappointment, tiredness, or pleasure.

good grief idiom 맙소사!, 세상에!
You can use 'good grief' for expressing surprise or disbelief.

Dr. Dan

1. What did Dr. Dan ask the Lambchops about their family?

A. He asked if the family knew how Stanley had gotten flat again.

B. He asked if the family could get rid of the bulletin board in their home.

C. He asked if other members of the family had ever become flat before.

D. He asked if other members of the family knew that Stanley was flat again.

2. What was written in the _Difficult and Peculiar Cases_ book?

A. Flatness was a very common condition.

B. The first case of sudden flatness had occurred many years ago.

C. There was a lot of documentation about flatness.

D. The first person to become flat eventually had become round again.

3. **What did Dr. Dan think had caused Stanley to become flat?**

   A. Stanley's young age and poor balance

   B. The shape of Stanley's upper torso

   C. The weakness of Stanley's skeleton

   D. The pressures created by the tennis ball and shelf corner

4. **How did Dr. Dan know so much about flatness?**

   A. He read a lot about the condition.

   B. He asked the world's leading authority on the OBP about it.

   C. He met many patients with the condition.

   D. He himself had become flat once.

5. **What would be dangerous, according to Dr. Dan?**

   A. Keeping Stanley flat forever

   B. Letting Stanley play outside

   C. Putting pressure on Stanley's OBP again

   D. Hitting Stanley outside of his OBP

Check Your Reading Speed

1분에 몇 단어를 읽는지 리딩 속도를 측정해보세요.

$$\frac{529 \text{ words}}{\text{reading time (\quad) sec}} \times 60 = (\qquad) \text{ WPM}$$

Build Your Vocabulary

* **widen** [waidn] v. 넓어지다; (정도·범위 등이) 커지다
If your eyes widen, they open more.

good heavens idiom 큰일이군!, 저런!
You say 'good heavens!' or 'heavens!' to express surprise or to emphasize that you agree or disagree with someone.

bulletin board [búlitən bɔːrd] n. 게시판
A bulletin board is a board which is usually attached to a wall in order to display notices giving information about something.

firm [fəːrm] a. 단단한; 단호한, 확고한 (firmly ad. 단단하게; 단호히)
If something is firm, it does not shake or move when you put weight or pressure on it, because it is strongly made or securely fastened.

be at a loss idiom 어쩔 줄을 모르다
If you say that you are at a loss, you mean that you do not know what to do in a particular situation.

account [əkáunt] v. 설명하다; n. 계좌; 설명; 기술
To account for something means to give an explanation for something bad that has happened, especially something that you are responsible for.

attack [ətǽk] n. 도짐, 발발; 폭행, 공격; v. 공격하다
An attack of an illness is a short period in which you suffer badly from it.

dress [dres] v. 옷을 입다; n. 드레스; 옷
When you dress or dress yourself, you put on clothes.

all of a sudden idiom 갑자기
If something happens all of a sudden, it happens quickly and unexpectedly.

frown [fraun] v. 얼굴을 찡그리다, 눈살을 찌푸리다; n. 찡그림, 찌푸림
When someone frowns, their eyebrows become drawn together, because they are annoyed or puzzled.

hit [hit] v. (hit–hit) 때리다; (생각 등이) 떠오르다; n. 치기, 강타
If you hit someone or something, you deliberately touch them with a lot of force, with your hand or an object held in your hand.

bang [bæŋ] v. 쿵 하고 찧다; 쾅 하고 치다; 쾅 하고 닫다; n. 쾅 (하는 소리)
If you bang a part of your body, you accidentally knock it against something and hurt yourself.

case [keis] n. 용기, 통, 상자; (특정한 상황의) 경우; 사건
A case is a container that is specially designed to hold or protect something.

peculiar [pikjúːljər] a. 기묘한, 이상한; 특유한, 고유의
If you describe someone or something as peculiar, you think that they are strange or unusual, sometimes in an unpleasant way.

extreme [ikstríːm] a. 극도의, 극심한; 지나친, 심각한; n. 극단
(extremely ad. 극도로, 극히)
You use extremely in front of adjectives and adverbs to emphasize that the specified quality is present to a very great degree.

rare [rɛər] a. 드문, 보기 힘든; 진귀한, 희귀한
An event or situation that is rare does not occur very often.

minimal [mínəməl] a. 아주 적은, 최소의
Something that is minimal is very small in quantity, value, or degree.

documentation [dàkjumentéiʃən] n. 기록, 문서화; 서류
Documentation consists of documents which provide proof or evidence of something, or are a record of something.

hearsay [híərsei] n. 전해 들은 말
Hearsay is information which you have been told but do not know to be true.

report [ripɔ́ːrt] n. (사실 여부가 불분명한) 이야기; 기록, 보고; 보도;
v. 알리다, 발표하다, 전하다; (신문·방송에서) 보도하다
If you say that there are reports that something has happened, you mean that some people say it has happened but you have no direct evidence of it.

date [deit] v. ~의 연대를 추정하다; 날짜를 적다;
n. (특정한) 날짜; (과거나 미래의 어느) 시기; (만나기로 하는) 약속
If you date something, you give or discover the date when it was made or when it began.

century [séntʃəri] n. 세기; 100년
A century is a period of a hundred years that is used when stating a date. For example, the 19th century was the period from 1801 to 1900.

battle [bǽtl] n. 전투; 투쟁; v. 싸우다, 투쟁하다
A battle is a violent fight between groups of people, especially one between military forces during a war.

fierce [fiərs] a. 사나운, 험악한; 격렬한, 맹렬한
A fierce animal or person is very aggressive or angry.

aide [eid] n. 부관; 보좌관
An aide is an assistant to someone who has an important job, especially in government or in the armed forces.

strike [straik] v. (struck–struck/stricken) (세게) 치다, 부딪치다; (갑자기) 공격하다;
n. 공격; 치기, 때리기
If you strike someone or something, you deliberately hit them.

* **simultaneous** [sàiməltéiniəs] a. 동시에 일어나는, 동시의
(simultaneously ad. 동시에)
Things which are simultaneous happen or exist at the same time.

at once idiom 즉시; 동시에
If you do something at once, you do it immediately.

* **shield** [ʃi:ld] n. 방패; 보호 장치; v. 보호하다, 가리다
A shield is a large piece of metal or leather which soldiers used to carry
to protect their bodies while they were fighting.

복습 **plate** [pleit] n. 판; 접시, 그릇; (자동차) 번호판
A plate is a flat piece of metal, especially on machinery or a building.

* **regain** [rigéin] v. 되찾다, 회복하다; 되돌아오다
If you regain something that you have lost, you get it back again.

girth [gə:rθ] n. 둘레 치수; 허리둘레
The girth of a thick or fat object, like a tree or a body, is the distance
around its outside.

* **suspect** [səspékt] v. 의심하다; 수상쩍어 하다; n. 용의자
You use suspect when you are stating something that you believe is
probably true, in order to make it sound less strong or direct.

* **beg** [beg] v. 간청하다, 애원하다; 구걸하다
If you beg someone to do something, you ask them very anxiously or
eagerly to do it.

‡ **pardon** [pa:rdn] int. 뭐라고요; n. 용서; v. 용서하다 (beg pardon idiom 뭐라고요)
You say 'I beg your pardon?' when you want someone to repeat what
they have just said because you have not heard or understood it.

osteal [ástiəl] a. (= osseous) 뼈로 이루어진; 뼈가 된
Oteal means of or relating to bone or to the skeleton.

anatomy [ənǽtəmi] n. (해부학적) 구조; 해부학 (anatomical a. 해부학상의, 해부의)
Anatomical means relating to the structure of the bodies of people and animals.

feature [fí:tʃər] n. 특징, 특성; v. 특별히 포함하다, 특징으로 삼다
A feature of something is an interesting or important part or characteristic of it.

complex [kəmpléks] a. 복잡한; n. 복합 건물, (건물) 단지
Something that is complex has many different parts, and is therefore often difficult to understand.

miracle [mírəkl] n. 기적 (같은 일)
If you say that a good event is a miracle, you mean that it is very surprising and unexpected.

skeleton [skélətn] n. 골격; 해골; (건물 등의) 뼈대
Your skeleton is the framework of bones in your body.

delicate [délikət] a. 정교한; 연약한; 섬세한, 우아한
A delicate task, movement, action, or product needs or shows great skill and attention to detail.

framework [fréimwə:rk] n. 뼈대, 골조
A framework is a structure that forms a support or frame for something.

support [səpɔ́:rt] n. 지탱함; 지지, 지원; v. 지지하다; 지원하다; 떠받치다
A support is something that holds the weight of an object, building, or structure so that it does not move or fall.

occur [əkə́:r] v. (어디에) 존재하다; 일어나다, 발생하다
When something occurs in a particular place, it exists or is present there.

torso [tɔ́:rsou] n. 몸통
Your torso is the main part of your body, and does not include your head, arms, and legs.

* **vulnerable** [vʌ́lnərəbl] a. 취약한, 연약한
Something that is vulnerable can be easily harmed or affected by something bad.

* **apply** [əplái] v. (손·발 등으로) 누르다; 적용하다; 신청하다
(application n. (열·힘 등을) 가함)
The application of something to a surface is the act or process of putting it on or rubbing it into the surface.

* **pressure** [préʃər] n. 압력; 압박(감), 스트레스; v. 강요하다; 압력을 가하다
Pressure is force that you produce when you press hard on something.

* **vary** [véəri] v. 달라지다; 서로 다르다
If something varies or if you vary it, it becomes different or changed.

* **depend** [dipénd] v. ~에 달려 있다, 좌우되다; 의지하다
You use depending on when you are saying that something varies according to the circumstances mentioned.

* **particular** [pərtíkjulər] a. 특정한; 특별한; 까다로운
You use particular to emphasize that you are talking about one thing or one kind of thing rather than other similar ones.

* **design** [dizáin] n. 계획, 의도; 설계; v. 설계하다
A design is a general plan or intention that someone has in their mind when they are doing something.

let us say idiom 그러니까, 예를 들면
You can use say or let us say when you mention something as an example.

* **individual** [ìndəvídʒuəl] n. 개인; 개성 있는 사람; a. 각각의; 개인의
An individual is a person.

* **involve** [inválv] v. 관련시키다, 연루시키다; 수반하다, 포함하다
If a situation or activity involves someone, they are taking part in it.

복습 shelf [ʃelf] n. 선반; (책장의) 칸
A shelf is a flat piece of wood, metal, or glass which is attached to a wall
or to the sides of a cupboard.

affect [əfékt] v. 영향을 미치다; (강한 정서적) 충격을 주다
If something affects a person or thing, it influences them or causes them
to change in some way.

thereby [ðɛərbái] ad. 그렇게 함으로써, 그것 때문에
You use thereby to introduce an important result or consequence of the
event or action you have just mentioned.

puzzle [pʌzl] v. 어리둥절하게 하다; n. 퍼즐; 수수께끼
(puzzled a. 어리둥절해하는, 얼떨떨한)
Someone who is puzzled is confused because they do not understand
something.

remarkable [rimá:rkəbl] a. 놀랄 만한, 놀라운, 주목할 만한
(remarkably ad. 몹시, 매우)
Someone or something that is remarkable is unusual or special in a way
that makes people notice them and be surprised or impressed.

inform [infɔ́:rm] v. 알아내다; 알리다, 통지하다 (informed a. 잘 아는)
Someone who is informed knows about a subject or what is happening
in the world.

read up on idiom ~에 관하여 많이 공부하다
To read up on something means to read a lot about a particular subject
in order to learn about it.

복습 sigh [sai] v. 한숨을 쉬다, 한숨짓다; 탄식하듯 말하다; n. 한숨
When you sigh, you let out a deep breath, as a way of expressing feelings
such as disappointment, tiredness, or pleasure.

seek [si:k] v. 찾다; 청하다, 구하다
When someone seeks something, they try to obtain it.

leading [líːdiŋ] a. 가장 중요한, 선두적인
The leading person or thing in a particular area is the one which is most important or successful.

authority [əθɔ́ːrəti] n. 권위자; 지휘권; 권한
Someone who is an authority on a particular subject knows a lot about it.

motion [móuʃən] v. (손·머리로) 몸짓을 해 보이다; n. 운동; 동작, 몸짓
If you motion to someone, you move your hand or head as a way of telling them to do something or telling them where to go.

put through idiom 겪게 하다
To put someone through something means to force them to do something difficult or unpleasant.

lad [læd] n. 사내애; 청년
A lad is a young man or boy.

skeletal [skélitl] a. 뼈대의; 해골 같은
Skeletal means relating to the bones in your body.

strain [strein] n. 압력, 압박; 부담, 압박감; 염좌; v. 안간힘을 쓰다; 한계에 이르게 하다
Strain is a force that pushes, pulls, or stretches something in a way that may damage it.

stick [stik] n. 막대기, 나무토막; v. 찌르다, 박다; 붙이다, 붙다
A stick is a long thin piece of wood which is used for a particular purpose.

Stanley Sails

1. What is a spinnaker used for?

    A. It is used to block wind.

    B. It is used to create wind.

    C. It is used to make a boat go slower.

    D. It is used to make a boat go faster.

2. Why did Mr. Jones want to beat Jasper Green?

    A. Jasper Green had been unkind to him once.

    B. Jasper Green thought he was better than everyone else.

    C. He didn't like Jasper Green's boat.

    D. He had lost many races to Jasper Green.

3. **How did Stanley feel after the race started?**

   A. He felt anxious.

   B. He felt relaxed.

   C. He felt ill.

   D. He felt busy.

4. **What did NOT happen after the spinnaker ripped?**

   A. *Lovebug* became slower.

   B. The mainsail fell down.

   C. The spinnaker could not be used anymore.

   D. Stanley became the spinnaker.

5. **What did the race committee say about *Lovebug*?**

   A. *Lovebug* had crossed the finish line last.

   B. *Lovebug* was not the first boat to use a person as a sail.

   C. *Lovebug* had won the race fairly.

   D. A crew member should not have been used as a sail on

   Lovebug.

1분에 몇 단어를 읽는지 리딩 속도를 측정해보세요.

$$\frac{1{,}099 \text{ words}}{\text{reading time (\quad) sec}} \times 60 = (\quad) \text{ WPM}$$

Build Your Vocabulary

sail [seil] v. 항해하다; 미끄러지듯 나아가다; n. 돛
If you sail a boat or if a boat sails, it moves across water using its sails.

college [kálidʒ] n. 대학(교)
A college is an institution where students study for degrees and where academic research is done.

remind [rimáind] v. 상기시키다, 다시 한 번 알려 주다
If someone reminds you of a fact or event that you already know about, they say something which makes you think about it.

date [deit] n. (만나기로 하는) 약속; (특정한) 날짜; (과거나 미래의 어느) 시기;
v. ~의 연대를 추정하다; 날짜를 적다
A date is an appointment to meet someone or go out with them.

hesitate [hézətèit] v. 망설이다, 주저하다; 거리끼다
If you hesitate, you do not speak or act for a short time, usually because you are uncertain, embarrassed, or worried about what you are going to say or do.

mention [ménʃən] v. 말하다, 언급하다; n. 언급, 거론
If you mention something, you say something about it, usually briefly.

get over idiom ~을 극복하다
If you get over something, you start to feel happy or well again after something bad has happened to you.

pick up idiom ~를 (차에) 태우러 가다; 더 강해지다

If you pick someone up, you go and meet someone that you have
arranged to take somewhere in a vehicle.

seashore [síːʃɔːr] n. 해안

The seashore is the part of a coast where the land slopes down into
the sea.

inquire [inkwáiər] v. 묻다, 알아보다

If you inquire about something, you ask for information about it.

foreign [fɔ́ːrən] a. 외국의

Something or someone that is foreign comes from or relates to a country
that is not your own.

kingdom [kíŋdəm] n. 왕국

A kingdom is a country or region that is ruled by a king or queen.

amaze [əméiz] v. (대단히) 놀라게 하다; 경악하게 하다 (amazing a. 놀라운)

You say that something is amazing when it is very surprising and makes
you feel pleasure, approval, or wonder.

recall [rikɔ́ːl] v. 기억해 내다, 상기하다; 다시 불러들이다; n. 회상

When you recall something, you remember it and tell others about it.

harbor [háːrbər] n. 항구, 항만; 피난처

A harbor is an area of the sea at the coast which is partly enclosed by
land or strong walls, so that boats can be left there safely.

rudder [rʌ́dər] n. [항해] (배의) 키

A rudder is a device for steering a boat. It consists of a vertical piece of
wood or metal at the back of the boat.

steer [stiər] v. (보트·자동차 등을) 조종하다; (특정 방향으로) 움직이다

When you steer a car, boat, or plane, you control it so that it goes in the
direction that you want.

⋆**zip** [zip] n. 지퍼; v. 지퍼를 잠그다; (어떤 방향으로) 쌩 하고 가다
(zip bag n. 지퍼가 달린 가방)
A zip or zip fastener is a device used to open and close parts of clothes and bags.

run before the wind idiom (배가) 순풍을 받고 달리다
If a boat runs before the wind, it moves in the same direction as the wind, so as to travel more quickly.

⋆**puff** [pʌf] v. 부풀어오르다; (담배 등을) 뻐끔뻐끔 피우다; n. (담배 등을) 피우기
To puff out means to make something larger and rounder by filling it with air.

go on idiom 말을 계속하다; (어떤 상황이) 계속되다
If you go on, you continue speaking after a short pause.

⋆**committee** [kəmíti] n. 위원회
A committee is a group of people who meet to make decisions or plans for a larger group or organization that they represent.

⋆**judge** [dʒʌdʒ] n. 심판, 심사위원; 판사; v. 판단하다; 심판을 보다
A judge is a person who decides who will be the winner of a competition.

buoy [buːi] n. 부표; v. 기분을 좋게 하다; ~을 (물에) 뜨게 하다
A buoy is a floating object that is used to show ships and boats where they can go and to warn them of danger.

race [reis] n. 경주; 경쟁; 인종, 종족; v. 쏜살같이 가다; 경주하다
A race is a competition to see who is the fastest, for example in running, swimming, or driving.

⋆**cast** [kæst] v. (cast-cast) (힘껏) 던지다; (시선·미소 등을) 던지다; n. 출연자들
(cast off idiom (출항을 위해) 밧줄을 풀어 던지다)
To cast off means to untie the rope fastening your boat to the land so that you can sail away.

moor [muər] v. (배를) 계류하다, 정박하다; n. 황야 지대, 황무지
(mooring n. (pl.) (배의) 계류용 밧줄)
If you moor a boat somewhere, you stop and tie it to the land with a
rope or chain so that it cannot move away.

⁎ **beat** [bi:t] v. (게임·시합에서) 이기다; 때리다; n. 리듬; 고동, 맥박
If you beat someone in a competition or election, you defeat them.

never mind idiom 신경쓰지 마, 괜찮아
You use 'never mind' to tell someone that they need not do something
or worry about something, because it is not important or because you
will do it yourself.

⁎ **friendly** [fréndli] a. 상냥한, 다정한; (행동이) 친절한, 우호적인
If someone is friendly, they behave in a pleasant, kind way, and like to
be with other people.

⁎ **wave** [weiv] n. (손·팔을) 흔들기; 파도, 물결; v. (손·팔을) 흔들다; 흔들리다
A wave is a movement of your hand used for saying hello or goodbye
to someone or for giving a signal.

⁎ **ignore** [ignɔ́:r] v. (사람을) 못 본 척하다; 무시하다
If you ignore someone or something, you pay no attention to them.

⁎ **mood** [mu:d] n. 기분; 분위기
Your mood is the way you are feeling at a particular time. If you are in
a bad mood, you feel angry and impatient.

⁎ **pistol** [pístəl] n. 권총, 피스톨
A pistol is a small gun which is held in and fired from one hand.

⁎ **shot** [ʃat] n. 발사; (한 번) 치기; 시도; 사진
A shot is an act of firing a gun.

⁎ **signal** [sígnəl] v. (동작·소리로) 신호를 보내다; 암시하다; n. 신호; 징조
If someone or something signals an event, they suggest that the event
is happening or likely to happen.

glide [glaid] v. 미끄러지듯 움직이다; 활강하다; n. 미끄러지는 듯한 움직임
If you glide somewhere, you move silently and in a smooth and effortless way.

mark [ma:rk] v. 표시하다; 자국을 내다; n. 자국, 흔적
If something marks a place or position, it shows where something else is or where it used to be.

streamer [strí:mər] n. (장식용) 색 테이프
Streamers are long rolls of colored paper used for decorating rooms at parties.

sit back idiom 편안히 앉다; (관여하지 않고) 가만히 있다
If you sit back, you get into a comfortable position, for example in a chair, and relax.

breeze [bri:z] n. 산들바람, 미풍
A breeze is a gentle wind.

cheerful [ʧíərfəl] a. 발랄한, 쾌활한; 쾌적한
Something that is cheerful is pleasant and makes you feel happy.

crackle [krækl] v. 탁탁 소리를 내다; n. 탁탁 하는 소리
If something crackles, it makes a rapid series of short, harsh noises.

billow [bílou] v. 부풀어 오르다; (연기 등이) 피어오르다; n. 자욱하게 피어오르는 것
When something made of cloth billows, it swells out and moves slowly in the wind.

shore [ʃɔ:r] n. 기슭, 해안, 호숫가
The shores or the shore of a sea, lake, or wide river is the land along the edge of it.

porch [pɔ:rʧ] n. (건물 입구에 있는) 현관
A porch is a sheltered area at the entrance to a building. It has a roof and sometimes has walls.

★ **faint** [feint] a. 희미한, 약한; v. 실신하다, 기절하다; n. 기절 (faintly ad. 희미하게)
A faint sound, color, mark, feeling, or quality has very little strength or intensity.

way to go idiom 잘 한다!, 잘 했어!
People say 'way to go' to encourage someone to continue the good work.

★ **sailor** [séilər] n. 선원, 뱃사람
A sailor is someone who works on a ship or sails a boat.

★ **tease** [ti:z] v. 놀리다, 장난하다; (동물을) 못 살게 굴다; n. 장난, 놀림
To tease someone means to laugh at them or make jokes about them in order to embarrass, annoy, or upset them.

abreast [əbrést] ad. 나란히
If people or things walk or move abreast, they are next to each other, side by side, and facing in the same direction.

hoist [hɔist] v. 들어올리다, 끌어올리다; n. 끌어올리기
If you hoist something heavy somewhere, you lift it or pull it up there.

⁑ **round** [raund] v. (모퉁이·커브 등을) 돌다; a. 둥근, 동그란; ad. 여기저기, 도처에;
n. 한 차례
If you round a place or obstacle, you move in a curve past the edge or corner of it.

★ **exclaim** [ikskléim] v. 소리치다, 외치다
If you exclaim, you cry out suddenly in surprise, strong emotion, or pain.

★ **attach** [ətǽʧ] v. 붙이다, 첨부하다; 연관되다
If you attach something to an object, you join it or fasten it to the object.

★ **mast** [mæst] n. [항해] (배의) 돛대
The masts of a boat are the tall upright poles that support its sails.

whoosh [hwu:ʃ] n. 쉭 하는 소리; v. (아주 빠르게) 휙 하고 지나가다
People sometimes say 'whoosh' when they are emphasizing the fact that something happens very suddenly or very fast.

★ **surge** [səːrdʒ] v. (재빨리) 밀려들다; n. (갑자기) 밀려듦; (감정이) 치밀어 오름
If a crowd of people surge forward, they suddenly move forward together.

복습 **visible** [vízəbl] a. (눈에) 보이는, 알아볼 수 있는; 뚜렷한 (invisible a. 보이지 않는)
If you describe something as invisible, you mean that it cannot be seen, for example because it is transparent, hidden, or very small.

★ **rip** [rip] v. (갑자기) 찢어지다; (재빨리·거칠게) 떼어 내다; n. (길게) 찢어진 곳
When something rips or when you rip it, you tear it forcefully with your hands or with a tool such as a knife.

★ **tear** [tɛər] ① v. (tore-torn) 찢다, 뜯다; 뜯어 내다; n. 찢어진 곳, 구멍 ② n. 눈물
If you tear paper, cloth, or another material, or if it tears, you pull it into two pieces or you pull it so that a hole appears in it.

★ **streak** [striːk] v. 기다란 자국을 내다; 전속력으로 가다; n. 줄무늬
If something streaks a surface, it makes long stripes or marks on the surface.

★ **downward** [dáunwərd] ad. 아래쪽으로; a. 아래쪽으로 내려가는
If you move or look downward, you move or look toward the ground or a lower level.

★ **flap** [flæp] v. 펄럭거리다; 퍼덕거리다; n. 덮개; 퍼덕거림
If something such as a piece of cloth or paper flaps or if you flap it, it moves quickly up and down or from side to side.

★ **useless** [júːslis] a. 소용없는, 쓸모 없는 (uselessly ad. 쓸데없이, 헛되이)
If something is useless, you cannot use it.

tough luck idiom 거 참 운도 없군
You can say 'tough luck' to show that you do not feel sorry for someone who has a problem.

take hold of idiom ~을 잡다, 붙잡다
If you take hold of something, you have or take it in your hands.

38

that's it idiom 바로 그거야
You can use 'that's it' to tell someone that something is correct.

twist [twist] v. (고개·몸 등을) 돌리다; 휘다, 구부리다; n. (손으로) 돌리기
If you twist part of your body such as your head or your shoulders, you turn that part while keeping the rest of your body still.

grab [græb] v. (와락·단단히) 붙잡다; 급히 ~하다; n. 와락 잡아채려고 함
If you grab something, you take it or pick it up suddenly and roughly.

plant [plænt] v. (단단히) 두다; 자리를 잡다; n. 식물, 초목; 공장
If you plant something somewhere, you put it there firmly.

press [pres] v. 밀다; 누르다; (무엇에) 바짝 대다; n. 언론; 인쇄
If you press something somewhere, you push it firmly against something else.

chest [ʧest] ① n. 가슴, 흉부 ② n. 상자, 궤
Your chest is the top part of the front of your body where your ribs, lungs, and heart are.

butt [bʌt] n. 엉덩이; (무기·도구의) 뭉툭한 끝 부분; v. (머리로) 들이받다
Someone's butt is their bottom.

clubhouse [klʌ́bhaus] n. (스포츠) 클럽 회관
A clubhouse is a place where the members of a club, especially a sports club, meet.

admit [ædmít] v. 인정하다, 시인하다; 들어가게 하다
If you admit that something bad, unpleasant, or embarrassing is true, you agree, often unwillingly, that it is true.

complain [kəmpléin] v. 불평하다, 항의하다
If you complain about a situation, you say that you are not satisfied with it.

report [ripɔ́ːrt] v. 알리다, 발표하다, 전하다; (신문·방송에서) 보도하다;
n. 기록, 보고; 보도; (사실 여부가 불분명한) 이야기
If you report something that has happened, you tell people about it.

advise [ædváiz] v. 알리다; 조언하다, 충고하다

If you advise someone of a fact or situation, you tell them the fact or explain what the situation is.

crew [kru:] n. 조정 경기 팀; 승무원; v. (배의) 승무원을 하다

A crew is a team of people who row a boat in a race.

notice [nóutis] v. 알아채다, 인지하다; 주의하다; n. 신경 씀, 주목, 알아챔

If you notice something or someone, you become aware of them.

spill [spil] v. (액체를) 흘리다, 쏟다; 쏟아져 나오다; n. 흘린 액체, 유출물

If a liquid spills or if you spill it, it accidentally flows over the edge of a container.

close down idiom 가게를 닫다, 폐업하다

If a place such as a factory, shop, or school closes down, all work or activity stops there permanently.

slap [slæp] v. (손바닥으로) 철썩 때리다; 털썩 놓다; n. 철썩 때리기, 치기

If you slap someone, you hit them with the palm of your hand.

forehead [fɔ́:rhèd] n. 이마

Your forehead is the area at the front of your head between your eyebrows and your hair.

apologize [əpálədʒàiz] v. 사과하다

When you apologize to someone, you say that you are sorry that you have hurt them or caused trouble for them.

sake [seik] n. (~을) 위함 (for heaven's sake idiom 제발, 부디, 맙소사)

Some people use expressions such as 'for heaven's sake,' 'for God's sake,' or 'for goodness sake' in order to express annoyance or impatience, or to add force to a question or request.

don't give it another thought idiom 자꾸 생각할 필요 없어, 그만 됐어

You can use 'don't give it another thought' to tell someone not to worry when they have apologized for something.

Back to School

1. **How did Emma Weeks feel about Stanley being flat again?**

   A. She felt Stanley was just trying to get attention.

   B. She thought Stanley's flatness was interesting.

   C. She felt sorry for Stanley and his condition.

   D. She thought Stanley deserved to be flat.

2. **What did Flash Tobin assume about Stanley?**

   A. He assumed that Stanley missed being round.

   B. He assumed that Stanley hated being flat.

   C. He assumed that Stanley had been flat his whole life.

   D. He assumed that Stanley could become round whenever he wanted.

3. **Why did the soccer coach say that Stanley should maybe switch to another sport?**

   A. He didn't think Stanley was interested in soccer anymore.

   B. He didn't think Stanley was talented enough to play soccer.

   C. He thought Stanley preferred playing indoor sports.

   D. He thought Stanley would be safer playing an indoor sport.

4. **Why did Miss Elliott want Stanley to see the guidance counselor?**

   A. She was worried that Stanley was causing too much trouble.

   B. She saw that Stanley was not as happy as he used to be.

   C. She heard that the guidance counselor wanted to meet Stanley.

   D. She believed that the guidance counselor could help Stanley choose a new sport.

5. **What was one of the questions that Mr. Redfield asked Stanley?**

   A. He asked if Stanley knew how to become round again.

   B. He asked if a part of Stanley had hoped to become flat again.

   C. He asked if a part of Stanley was unhappy being on the soccer team.

   D. He asked if Stanley thought he would ever become round again.

1분에 몇 단어를 읽는지 리딩 속도를 측정해보세요.

$$\frac{776 \text{ words}}{\text{reading time (} \qquad \text{) sec}} \times 60 = (\qquad) \text{ WPM}$$

Build Your Vocabulary

★ **pleased** [pliːzd] a. 기쁜, 기뻐하는, 만족해하는

If you are pleased, you are happy about something or satisfied with something.

★ **classmate** [klǽsmeit] n. 급우, 반 친구

Your classmates are students who are in the same class as you at school or college.

⚓ **previous** [príːviəs] a. 앞의, 이전의

A previous event or thing is one that happened or existed before the one that you are talking about.

★ **fuss** [fʌs] n. 호들갑, 법석; 불평; v. 법석을 떨다; 안달하다
(make a fuss idiom 소란을 피우다)

If you make a fuss or kick up a fuss about something, you become angry or excited about it and complain.

복습 **cheerful** [ʧíərfəl] a. 발랄한, 쾌활한; 쾌적한

Something that is cheerful is pleasant and makes you feel happy.

⚓ **joke** [dʒouk] n. 농담; 웃음거리; v. 재미있는 이야기를 하다; 농담 삼아 말하다

A joke is something that is said or done to make you laugh, for example a funny story.

⚓ **mean** [miːn] a. 못된, 심술궂은; v. 의미하다

If you describe a person or animal as mean, you are saying that they are very bad-tempered and cruel.

*** pleasant** [plézənt] a. 상냥한; 즐거운, 기분 좋은 (unpleasant a. 기분 나쁜, 무례한)
An unpleasant person is very unfriendly and rude.

show-off [ʃóu-ɔːf] n. 과시적인 사람, 자랑쟁이
If you say that someone is a show-off, you are criticizing them for trying
to impress people by showing in a very obvious way what they can do
or what they own.

*** unusual** [ʌnjúːʒuəl] a. 특이한, 흔치 않은; 색다른 (unusually ad. 특이하게)
You can use unusually to suggest that something is not what normally
happens.

. investigate [invéstəgèit] v. 조사하다, 살피다; 연구하다
If someone, especially an official, investigates an event, situation, or
claim, they try to find out what happened or what is the truth.

*** field** [fiːld] n. 경기장; 들판, 밭
A sports field is an area of grass where sports are played.

*** post** [poust] n. 기둥, 말뚝; 우편; v. 배치하다, 파견하다 (goal post n. 골대)
A goal post is one of the two upright wooden posts that are connected
by a crossbar and form the goal in games such as football and rugby.

*** nod** [nad] v. (고개를) 끄덕이다, 까딱하다; n. (고개를) 끄덕임
If you nod, you move your head downward and upward to show that you
are answering 'yes' to a question, or to show agreement, understanding,
or approval.

sneak thief [sníːk θiːf] n. 좀도둑
A sneak thief is a person who steals paltry articles from premises, which
they enter through open doors or windows.

back and forth idiom 왔다 갔다; 앞뒤로; 좌우로; 여기저기에
If someone moves back and forth, they repeatedly move in one direction
and then in the opposite direction.

. impress [imprés] v. 깊은 인상을 주다, 감동을 주다 (impressed a. 감명을 받은)
If something impresses you, you feel great admiration for it.

shot [ʃat] n. 사진; 발사; (한 번) 치기; 총성; 시도
A shot is a photograph or a particular sequence of pictures in a film.

pump [pʌmp] n. 펌프; 펌프 사용; v. (펌프로) 퍼 올리다; (거세게) 솟구치다
(bicycle pump n. 자전거 공기 주입 펌프)
A pump is a machine or device that is used to force a liquid or gas to flow in a particular direction.

jealous [dʒéləs] a. 질투하는; 시샘하는 (jealousy n. 질투)
Jealousy is the feeling of anger or bitterness which someone has when they wish that they could have the qualities or possessions that another person has.

worrisome [wə́:risəm] a. 걱정스럽게 하는, 걱정스러운
Something that is worrisome causes people to worry.

coach [koutʃ] n. (스포츠 팀의) 코치; v. 지시하다; 코치하다
A coach is someone who trains a person or team of people in a particular sport.

sake [seik] n. (~을) 위함 (for the sake of idiom ~때문에)
When you do something for the sake of someone, you do it in order to help them or make them happy.

switch [switʃ] v. 전환하다, 바꾸다; n. 스위치; 전환
If you switch to something different, for example to a different system, task, or subject of conversation, you change to it from what you were doing or saying before.

indoor [índɔ:r] a. 실내의, 실내용의
Indoor activities or things are ones that happen or are used inside a building and not outside.

notice [nóutis] v. 알아채다, 인지하다; 주의하다; n. 신경 씀, 주목, 알아챔
If you notice something or someone, you become aware of them.

guidance [gaidns] n. 지도, 안내
Guidance is help and advice.

⋆ **counsel** [káunsəl] v. 상담을 하다; 충고하다; n. 조언
(guidance counselor n. 생활 지도 교사)
A guidance counselor is a person who works in a school giving students advice about careers and personal problems.

⋮ **trouble** [trʌbl] v. 괴롭히다, 애 먹이다; n. 문제, 곤란, 골칫거리
(troubled a. 걱정하는, 불안해하는)
Someone who is troubled is worried because they have problems.

⋮ **lean** [li:n] v. 기울이다, (몸을) 숙이다; ~에 기대다; a. 군살이 없는, 호리호리한
When you lean in a particular direction, you bend your body in that direction.

⋆ **confidential** [kànfədénʃəl] a. 비밀의; 은밀한
Information that is confidential is meant to be kept secret or private.

⋮ **lower** [lóuər] v. 낮추다; ~을 내리다
If you lower your voice or if your voice lowers, you speak more quietly.

⋆ **pad** [pæd] n. 메모장; 보호대; v. 완충재를 대다
A pad of paper is a number of pieces of paper which are fixed together along the top or the side, so that each piece can be torn off when it has been used.

복습 **admit** [ædmít] v. 인정하다, 시인하다; 들어가게 하다
If you admit that something bad, unpleasant, or embarrassing is true, you agree, often unwillingly, that it is true.

no way idiom 절대로 아니다; 절대로 안 돼, 싫어
You can say 'no way' as an emphatic way of saying 'no.'

복습 **firm** [fə:rm] a. 단호한, 확고한; 단단한 (firmly ad. 단호히; 단단하게)
If you describe someone as firm, you mean they behave in a way that shows that they are not going to change their mind, or that they are the person who is in control.

⋆ **kite** [kait] n. 연
A kite is an object, usually used as a toy, which is flown in the air.

tired [taiərd] a. (~에) 싫증난; 피곤한, 지친 (get tired of idiom 싫증이 나다)
If you are tired of something, you do not want it to continue because you are bored of it or unhappy with it.

pleasure [pléʒər] n. 기쁨, 즐거움
If something gives you pleasure, you get a feeling of happiness, satisfaction, or enjoyment from it.

sail [seil] n. 돛; v. 항해하다; 미끄러지듯 나아가다
Sails are large pieces of material attached to the mast of a ship. The wind blows against the sails and pushes the ship along.

race [reis] n. 경주; 경쟁; 인종, 종족; v. 쏜살같이 가다; 경주하다
A race is a competition to see who is the fastest, for example in running, swimming, or driving.

stare [stɛər] v. 빤히 쳐다보다, 응시하다; n. 빤히 쳐다보기, 응시
If you stare at someone or something, you look at them for a long time.

press [pres] v. 누르다; 밀다; (무엇에) 바짝 대다; n. 언론; 인쇄
If you press something somewhere, you push it firmly against something else.

fingertip [fíŋgərtip] n. 손가락 끝
Your fingertips are the ends of your fingers.

terrible [térəbl] a. 형편없는; 끔찍한, 소름끼치는; (나쁜 정도가) 극심한
If something is terrible, it is very bad or of very poor quality.

eyesight [áisàit] n. 시력, 시야
Your eyesight is your ability to see.

glance [glæns] v. 흘깃 보다; 대충 훑어보다; n. 흘깃 봄
If you glance at something or someone, you look at them very quickly and then look away again immediately.

time is up idiom 시간이 다 됐다, 시간이 끝났다
If a period of time is up, it has come to an end.

Why Me?

1. **What did Arthur tell Mr. and Mrs. Lambchop when they came into the room?**
   A. He said Stanley hadn't laughed at his joke.
   B. He said Stanley was being selfish.
   C. He said Stanley was upset.
   D. He said Stanley was going to eat fruit.

2. **How did Stanley feel about things always happening to him?**
   A. He felt it was unfair.
   B. He felt it was surprising.
   C. He felt it was funny.
   D. He felt it was natural.

3. **What did Arthur think about flatness and invisibility?**
   A. He was glad he had never experienced them.

   B. He thought they were annoying.

   C. He figured he would enjoy them.

   D. He agreed they caused many problems.

4. **What did Mr. Lambchop say about the reason that things happen?**
   A. The reason was often obvious at first.

   B. The reason was often not known until later.

   C. The reason was often not important.

   D. There was often no reason.

5. **How did Mr. and Mrs. Lambchop feel about Stanley?**
   A. They didn't know why Stanley was in such a bad mood.

   B. They understood why Stanley was upset.

   C. They didn't expect that anything else would happen to Stanley.

   D. They were proud that strange things had happened only to Stanley.

1분에 몇 단어를 읽는지 리딩 속도를 측정해보세요.

$$\frac{484 \text{ words}}{\text{reading time (} \quad \text{) sec}} \times 60 = (\quad) \text{ WPM}$$

Build Your Vocabulary

bedtime [bédtàim] n. 취침 시간, 잠자리에 드는 시간
Your bedtime is the time when you usually go to bed.

＊**cheer** [tʃiər] v. 응원하다, 힘을 북돋우다; 환호하다; n. 환호
If someone cheers up, or something cheers someone up, they start to feel happier.

snack [snæk] v. 간식을 먹다; n. 간식
If you snack, you eat something such as a chocolate bar between meals.

복습 **visible** [vízəbl] a. (눈에) 보이는, 알아볼 수 있는; 뚜렷한 (invisible a. 보이지 않는)
If you describe something as invisible, you mean that it cannot be seen, for example because it is transparent, hidden, or very small.

＊**consequence** [kánsəkwèns] n. (발생한 일의) 결과; 중요함
The consequences of something are the results or effects of it.

＊＊**cross** [krɔːs] a. 짜증난, 약간 화가 난; v. (가로질러) 건너다; n. 십자 기호
Someone who is cross is rather angry or irritated.

복습 **terrible** [térəbl] a. 형편없는; 끔찍한, 소름끼치는; (나쁜 정도가) 극심한
If something is terrible, it is very bad or of very poor quality.

복습 **mood** [muːd] n. 기분; 분위기
Your mood is the way you are feeling at a particular time. If you are in a bad mood, you feel angry and impatient.

* **pillow** [pílou] n. 베개
A pillow is a rectangular cushion which you rest your head on when you are in bed.

‡ **practical** [præktikəl] a. 거의 완전한, 사실상의; 현실적인; 타당한
(practically ad. 사실상, 거의)
Practically means almost, but not completely or exactly.

* **hush** [hʌʃ] v. ~을 조용히 시키다, 진정시키다; int. 쉿, 조용히 해
If you hush someone or if they hush, they stop speaking or making a noise.

복습 **dear** [diər] n. 얘야; 여보, 당신; int. 이런!; 맙소사!; a. 사랑하는; ~에게
You can call someone dear as a sign of affection.

복습 **trouble** [trʌbl] v. 괴롭히다, 애 먹이다; n. 문제, 곤란, 골칫거리
If something troubles you, it makes you feel rather worried.

put out idiom (불·전깃불 등을) 끄다
If you put out an electric light, you make it stop shining by pressing a switch.

* **overhead** [ouvərhéd] a. 머리 위의, 높이 세운; ad. 머리 위로, 하늘 높이
You use overhead to indicate that something is above you or above the place that you are talking about.

patter [pǽtər] n. 후두두 하는 소리; v. 후두두 하는 소리를 내다
A patter is a series of quick, quiet, tapping sounds.

* **glow** [glou] n. (은은한) 불빛; 홍조; v. 빛나다, 타다; (얼굴이) 상기되다
A glow is a dull, steady light, for example the light produced by a fire when there are no flames.

* **cozy** [kóuzi] a. 아늑한, 편안한; 친밀한
A house or room that is cosy is comfortable and warm.

after all idiom 결국에는; 어쨌든
You use after all when you are saying that something that you thought might not be the case is in fact the case.

‡put [put] v. 말하다, (말·글로) 옮기다; 놓다, 두다

When you put an idea or remark in a particular way, you express it in that way.

⋆squeeze [skwi:z] v. (꼭) 쥐다; (좁은 곳에) 비집고 들어가다; n. (손으로 꼭) 쥐기

If you squeeze something, you press it firmly, usually with your hands.

‡expect [ikspékt] v. 예상하다, 기대하다 (unexpected a. 예기치 않은, 예상 밖의)

If an event or someone's behavior is unexpected, it surprises you because you did not think that it was likely to happen.

‡upset [ʌpsét] v. 속상하게 하다; a. 속상한, 마음이 상한 (upsetting a. 속상하게 하는)

If something upsets you, it makes you feel worried or unhappy.

⋆tail [teil] n. (동물의) 꼬리; 끝부분; v. 미행하다

The tail of an animal, bird, or fish is the part extending beyond the end of its body.

⋆pat [pæt] v. 쓰다듬다; 가볍게 두드리다; n. 쓰다듬기, 토닥거리기

If you pat something or someone, you tap them lightly, usually with your hand held flat.

switch off idiom (스위치 등을 눌러서) ~을 끄다

If you switch off something like an electrical device, a machine or an engine, you stop it working by pressing a switch or a button.

⋆darken [dá:rkən] v. 어두워지다; 우울해지다

A darkened building or room has no lights on inside it.

get it idiom 이해하다; 야단맞다, 벌받다

To get it means to understand an argument or the person making it.

⋆chuckle [ʧʌkl] v. 킬킬 웃다; 빙그레 웃다; n. 킬킬거림; 속으로 웃기

When you chuckle, you laugh quietly.

Emma

1. **What happened to most of the Merker Department Store?**

    A. It was torn down by workmen.

    B. It was hit by rubble.

    C. It was wrecked by bad weather.

    D. It fell down by itself.

2. **Why did Fire Chief Johnson forbid any rescue efforts to save Emma Weeks?**

    A. He said all of the wreckage needed to be removed first.

    B. He said nobody knew yet if Emma was injured.

    C. He said Emma needed only food and water.

    D. He said rescue efforts might cause the rest of the building to fall down.

3. **How did Emma appear when the reporter talked to her?**
    A. She appeared grateful.
    B. She appeared hopeful.
    C. She appeared impatient.
    D. She appeared confused.

4. **Why did Chief Johnson think that Stanley could help Emma?**
    A. Stanley could fit through narrow openings because he was flat.
    B. Stanley was smaller and faster than the flat firemen.
    C. Stanley could hold up the building so that it didn't collapse.
    D. Stanley would be able to recognize Emma because he knew her from school.

5. **How did Mrs. Lambchop first react to the idea of Stanley helping Emma?**
    A. She was relieved that the idea seemed possible.
    B. She thought that the idea was excellent.
    C. She didn't think that the idea would work.
    D. She felt that the idea was too dangerous.

1분에 몇 단어를 읽는지 리딩 속도를 측정해보세요.

$$\frac{808 \ words}{reading \ time \ (\quad) \ sec} \times 60 = (\quad) \ WPM$$

Build Your Vocabulary

⭐ **department store** [dipá:rtmənt stɔ:r] n. 백화점
A department store is a large shop which sells many different kinds of goods.

⭐ **downtown** [dauntáun] ad. 시내에; n. 도심지; 상업 지구
Downtown places are in or toward the center of a large town or city, where the shops and places of business are.

복습 **empty** [émpti] v. (건물 등을) 나가게 하다; (그릇 등을) 비우다; a. 빈; 공허한
If someone empties a room or place, or if it empties, everyone that is in it goes away.

복습 **tear** [tɛər] ① v. (tore–torn) 찢다, 뜯다; 뜯어 내다; n. 찢어진 곳, 구멍
(tear down idiom (건물·담 등을) 허물다) ② n. 눈물
To tear down a building or a wall means to pull or knock it down.

switch on idiom (전등 등의) 스위치를 켜다
If you switch on something like an electrical device, a machine or an engine, you start it working by pressing a switch or a button.

⭐ **latest** [léitist] a. 최근의
You use latest to describe something that is the most recent thing of its kind.

복습 **collapse** [kəlǽps] n. (건물의) 붕괴; v. 붕괴되다, 무너지다; (의식을 잃고) 쓰러지다
Collapse is an occasion when a building or other structure falls down.

newscaster [njú:zkæstər] n. (라디오·텔레비전의) 뉴스 프로그램 진행자
A newscaster is a person who reads the news on the radio or on
television.

rubble [rʌbl] n. (허물어진 건물의) 돌무더기, 잔해
When a building is destroyed, the pieces of brick, stone, or other materials
that remain are referred to as rubble.

folk [fouk] n. (pl.) 여러분, 얘들아; (pl.) (일반적인) 사람들; (pl.) 부모
You can use folks as a term of address when you are talking to several
people.

workman [wə́:rkmən] n. (pl. workmen) (육체노동) 노동자, 일꾼
A workman is a man who works with his hands, for example building or
repairing houses or roads.

treat [tri:t] v. 치료하다; (특정한 태도로) 대하다; 대접하다; n. (대접하는) 특별한 것; 기쁨
When a doctor or nurse treats a patient or an illness, he or she tries to
make the patient well again.

minor [máinər] a. 작은, 가벼운
A minor illness or operation is not likely to be dangerous to someone's
life or health.

bruise [bru:z] n. 멍, 타박상; v. 멍이 생기다; 의기소침하게 하다
A bruise is an injury which appears as a purple mark on your body,
although the skin is not broken.

injury [índʒəri] n. 부상; (마음의) 상처, 피해
An injury is damage done to a person's or an animal's body.

report [ripɔ́:rt] v. 알리다, 발표하다, 전하다; (신문·방송에서) 보도하다;
n. 기록, 보고; 보도; (사실 여부가 불분명한) 이야기
If you report something that has happened, you tell people about it.

request [rikwést] v. 요청하다, 요구하다; n. 요청; 요구 사항
If you request someone to do something, you politely or formally ask
them to do it.

avoid [əvɔ́id] v. 피하다; 막다, 모면하다
If you avoid a person or thing, you keep away from them.

slip [slip] n. (작은 종이) 조각; (작은) 실수; v. 미끄러지다; 슬며시 가다
A slip of paper is a small piece of paper.

hold on idiom 기다려, 멈춰; (~을) 계속 잡고 있다
If you say 'hold on' to someone, you ask them to wait or stop for a short time.

trap [træp] v. (위험한 장소·궁지에) 가두다; (함정으로) 몰아넣다; n. 덫, 올가미; 함정
If you are trapped somewhere, something falls onto you or blocks your way and prevents you from moving or escaping.

wreckage [rékidʒ] n. 잔해
When something such as a plane, car, or building has been destroyed, you can refer to what remains as wreckage or the wreckage.

local [lóukəl] a. 지역의, 현지의; n. 주민, 현지인
Local means existing in or belonging to the area where you live, or to the area that you are talking about.

businessman [bíznismæn] n. 실업가, 사업가
A businessman is a man who works in business.

exclaim [ikskléim] v. 소리치다, 외치다
If you exclaim, you cry out suddenly in surprise, strong emotion, or pain.

no wonder idiom ~하는 것도 당연하다
You can say 'no wonder' when you find out the reason for something that has been puzzling you for some time.

appear [əpíər] v. ~인 것 같다; 나타나다, 보이기 시작하다; 생기다, 발생하다
If you say that something appears to be the way you describe it, you are reporting what you believe or what you have been told, though you cannot be sure it is true.

fireman [fáiərmən] n. (pl. firemen) 소방관, 소방대원
A fireman is a person whose job is to put out fires.

scene [siːn] n. 현장; 장면, 광경; 풍경

The scene of an event is the place where it happened.

chink [tʃiŋk] n. 틈; 가늘게 새어 드는 빛; v. 쟁그랑거리다

A chink in a surface is a very narrow crack or opening in it.

demand [diménd] v. 요구하다; 강력히 묻다, 따지다; n. 요구; 수요

If you demand something such as information or action, you ask for it in a very forceful way.

chief [tʃiːf] n. (조직·집단의) 장(長); a. (계급·직급상) 최고위자인

The chief of an organization is the person who is in charge of it.

forbid [fərbíd] v. (forbade–forbidden) 금하다; ~을 어렵게 하다

If you forbid someone to do something, or if you forbid an activity, you order that it must not be done.

rescue [réskjuː] n. 구출, 구조, 구제; v. 구하다, 구출하다

A rescue is an attempt to save someone from a dangerous or unpleasant situation.

effort [éfərt] n. (조직적인) 활동; 수고; 노력, 공

An effort is a particular series of activities that is organized by a group of people in order to achieve something.

disturb [distə́ːrb] v. 건드리다; (작업·수면 등을) 방해하다; 불안하게 하다
(disturbance n. 어긋남)

Disturbance means upsetting or disorganizing something which was previously in a calm and well-ordered state.

shift [ʃift] v. (장소를) 옮기다; (견해·방식을) 바꾸다; n. 변화

If you shift something or if it shifts, it moves slightly.

rest [rest] n. 나머지; 휴식; v. 쉬다; 놓이다, (~에) 있다

The rest is used to refer to all the parts of something or all the things in a group that remain or that you have not already mentioned.

☆ **crash** [kræʃ] v. 박살나다; 충돌하다; 굉음을 내다; n. (자동차·항공기) 사고; 요란한 소리
(crash down idiom 부서지다, 붕괴하다)
If a building or a wall crashes down, it falls with a very loud noise.

☆ **screen** [skriːn] n. (텔레비전·컴퓨터) 화면; v. 가리다, 차단하다
A screen is a flat vertical surface on which pictures or words are shown.

⋅ **reporter** [ripɔ́ːrtər] n. (보도) 기자, 리포터
A reporter is someone who writes news articles or who broadcasts news reports.

⋅ **wreck** [rek] v. 망가뜨리다, 파괴하다; 난파시키다; n. 난파선; 잔해 (wrecked a. 망가진)
To wreck something means to completely destroy or ruin it.

☆ **crack** [kræk] n. (좁은) 틈; (갈라져 생긴) 금; v. 깨뜨리다; 갈라지다, 금이 가다
A crack is a very narrow gap between two things, or between two parts of a thing.

복습 **faint** [feint] a. 희미한, 약한; v. 실신하다, 기절하다; n. 기절
A faint sound, color, mark, feeling, or quality has very little strength or intensity.

복습 **sigh** [sai] v. 한숨을 쉬다, 한숨짓다; 탄식하듯 말하다; n. 한숨
When you sigh, you let out a deep breath, as a way of expressing feelings such as disappointment, tiredness, or pleasure.

⋅ **unfortunate** [ʌnfɔ́ːrtʃənət] a. 당혹스러운, 불쾌한; 운이 없는, 불행한
If you describe something that has happened as unfortunate, you think that it is inappropriate, embarrassing, awkward, or undesirable.

⋅ **tone** [toun] n. 어조; 음조, 음색
Someone's tone is a quality in their voice which shows what they are feeling or thinking.

복습 **strain** [strein] n. 부담, 압박감; 압력, 압박; 염좌; v. 안간힘을 쓰다; 한계에 이르게 하다
Strain is a state of worry and tension caused by a difficult situation.

supper [sʌ́pər] n. 저녁 식사

Some people refer to the main meal eaten in the early part of the evening as supper.

siren [sáiərən] n. (신호·경보) 사이렌

A siren is a warning device which makes a long, loud noise.

die away idiom 서서히 잦아들다

If a sound dies away, it gradually becomes weaker or fainter and finally disappears completely.

front door [frʌnt dɔ́:r] n. 현관

The front door of a house or other building is the main door, which is usually in the wall that faces a street.

department [dipá:rtmənt] n. 부서 (fire department n. 소방국)

The fire department is an organization which has the job of putting out fires.

curb [kə:rb] n. 도로 경계석, (차도 가의) 연석; v. 억제하다

The curb is the raised edge of a pavement or sidewalk which separates it from the road.

doorstep [dɔ́:rstep] n. 문간(의 계단)

A doorstep is a step in front of a door on the outside of a building.

get to the point idiom 요점을 말하다

When someone gets to the point, they start talking about the thing that is most important to them.

reckon [rékən] v. (~라고) 생각하다; 여겨지다

If you reckon that something is true, you think that it is true.

dreadful [drédfəl] a. 끔찍한, 지독한; 무시무시한 (dreadfully ad. 몹시, 굉장히)

Dreadful is used to emphasize the degree or extent of something bad.

policeman [pəlí:smən] n. 경찰관

A policeman is a person who is a member of the police force.

dig [dig] v. (구멍 등을) 파다; (무엇을 찾기 위해) 뒤지다; n. 쿡 찌르기
If people or animals dig, they make a hole in the ground or in a pile of earth, stones, or rubbish.

fella [félə] n. 남자; 남자 친구
You can refer to a man as a fella.

squeeze [skwi:z] v. (좁은 곳에) 비집고 들어가다; (꼭) 쥐다; n. (손으로 꼭) 쥐기
If you squeeze a person or thing somewhere or if they squeeze there, they manage to get through or into a small space.

narrow [nǽrou] a. 좁은; v. 좁아지다
Something that is narrow measures a very small distance from one side to the other, especially compared to its length or height.

opening [óupəniŋ] n. 구멍, 틈; 시작
An opening is a hole or empty space through which things or people can pass.

recollect [rèkəlékt] v. 기억해 내다, 생각해 내다
If you recollect something, you remember it.

hit [hit] v. (hit-hit) (생각 등이) 떠오르다; 때리다; n. 치기, 강타
When a feeling or an idea hits you, it suddenly affects you or comes into your mind.

wiggle [wigl] v. 꿈틀꿈틀 움직이다; n. 꿈틀꿈틀 움직이기
If you wiggle something or if it wiggles, it moves up and down or from side to side in small quick movements.

terrible [térəbl] a. (나쁜 정도가) 극심한; 끔찍한, 소름끼치는; 형편없는
(terribly ad. 몹시, 극심하게)
You use terrible to emphasize the great extent or degree of something.

tad [tæd] n. 조금
You can use a tad in expressions such as a tad big or a tad small when you mean that it is slightly too big or slightly too small.

⭑**risky** [ríski] a. 위험한; 아슬아슬한
If an activity or action is risky, it is dangerous or likely to fail.

⭑**sob** [sab] v. 흐느끼다, 흐느껴 울다; n. 흐느껴 울기, 흐느낌
When someone sobs, they cry in a noisy way, breathing in short breaths.

⭒**bite** [bait] v. (bit−bitten) (이빨로) 물다; 베어 물다; n. 한 입; 물기
If you bite something, you use your teeth to cut into it, for example in order to eat it or break it.

⭒**lip** [lip] n. 입술
Your lips are the two outer parts of the edge of your mouth.

⭑**afterwards** [ǽftərwərdz] ad. 나중에, 그 뒤에
If you do something or if something happens afterwards, you do it or it happens after a particular event or time that has already been mentioned.

복습**all of a sudden** idiom 갑자기
If something happens all of a sudden, it happens quickly and unexpectedly.

복습**after all** idiom 결국에는; 어쨌든
You use after all when you are saying that something that you thought might not be the case is in fact the case.

stuck [stʌk] a. 갇힌; 움직일 수 없는, 꼼짝 못하는
If you are stuck in a place, you want to get away from it, but are unable to.

복습**nod** [nad] v. (고개를) 끄덕이다, 까딱하다; n. (고개를) 끄덕임
If you nod, you move your head downward and upward to show that you are answering 'yes' to a question, or to show agreement, understanding, or approval.

⭑**enormous** [inɔ́:rməs] a. 막대한, 거대한
Something that is enormous is extremely large in size or amount.

Where Are You, Emma?

1. **Why did Emma say "Bananas!" when Stanley called her name?**

   A. She wanted Stanley to bring her bananas.

   B. She didn't feel like saying "Here!" again.

   C. She thought Stanley had told her to say "Bananas!"

   D. She wasn't sure how to respond when she heard her name.

2. **How did Emma feel when she saw Stanley?**

   A. She felt mad that he hadn't arrived sooner.

   B. She felt guilty for having made fun of him.

   C. She felt disappointed that he had been sent.

   D. She felt thankful that he cared about her.

3. **What did Emma think of the food and drink that Stanley had brought?**

    A. She thought there was too much food and soda.

    B. She thought there was not enough food and soda.

    C. She was excited to eat the food and drink the soda.

    D. She didn't want to eat the food and drink the soda.

4. **Why had Emma gone into the building?**

    A. She hadn't seen the "Keep out!" and "Danger!" signs.

    B. She hadn't cared about the "Keep out!" and "Danger" signs.

    C. She had gotten lost around the area.

    D. She had been looking for the parking lot.

5. **How did Emma and Stanley escape from the wreckage?**

    A. They found a door that they could wiggle through.

    B. They got out the same way Stanley had come in.

    C. They crawled through a hole that Stanley had found.

    D. They followed Chief Johnson's voice to an exit.

Check Your Reading Speed

1분에 몇 단어를 읽는지 리딩 속도를 측정해보세요.

$$\frac{1,106 \text{ words}}{\text{reading time (} \quad \text{) sec}} \times 60 = (\quad) \text{ WPM}$$

Build Your Vocabulary

remain [riméin] n. (pl.) 남은 것, 나머지; v. 계속 ~이다; 남다
The remains of something are the parts of it that are left after most of it has been taken away or destroyed.

chief [tʃiːf] n. (조직·집단의) 장(長); a. (계급·직급상) 최고위자인
The chief of an organization is the person who is in charge of it.

rescue [réskjuː] n. 구출, 구조, 구제; v. 구하다, 구출하다
A rescue is an attempt to save someone from a dangerous or unpleasant situation.

attempt [ətémpt] n. 시도; v. 시도하다, 애써 해보다
If you make an attempt to do something, you try to do it, often without success.

supply [səplái] v. 공급하다, 제공하다; n. (pl.) 용품, 비품; 공급
If you supply someone with something that they want or need, you give them a quantity of it.

slice [slais] n. (얇게 썬) 조각; 부분, 몫; v. 베다; 자르다, 썰다
A slice of bread, meat, fruit, or other food is a thin piece that has been cut from a larger piece.

wrap [ræp] v. 포장하다; (무엇의 둘레를) 두르다; 둘러싸다; n. 포장지; 랩
When you wrap something, you fold paper or cloth tightly round it to cover it completely, for example in order to protect it or so that you can give it to someone as a present.

cigarette [sigərét] n. 담배
Cigarettes are small tubes of paper containing tobacco which people smoke.

case [keis] n. 용기, 통, 상자; (특정한 상황의) 경우; 사건
A case is a container that is specially designed to hold or protect something.

tape [teip] v. 테이프로 붙이다; 끈으로 묶다; 녹음하다; n. (접착용) 테이프
If you tape one thing to another, you attach it using sticky tape.

packet [pǽkit] n. 통, 갑; 소포; 한 묶음
A packet is a small container in which a quantity of something is sold.

chest [ʧest] ① n. 가슴, 흉부 ② n. 상자, 궤
Your chest is the top part of the front of your body where your ribs, lungs, and heart are.

flashlight [flǽʃlait] n. 손전등
A flashlight is a small electric light which gets its power from batteries and which you can carry in your hand.

crack [kræk] n. (좁은) 틈; (갈라져 생긴) 금; v. 깨뜨리다; 갈라지다, 금이 가다
A crack is a very narrow gap between two things, or between two parts of a thing.

wreckage [rékidʒ] n. 잔해
When something such as a plane, car, or building has been destroyed, you can refer to what remains as wreckage or the wreckage.

fella [félə] n. 남자; 남자 친구
You can refer to a man as a fella.

holler [hálər] v. 소리지르다, 고함치다
If you holler, you shout loudly.

faint [feint] a. 희미한, 약한; v. 실신하다, 기절하다; n. 기절 (faintly ad. 희미하게)
A faint sound, color, mark, feeling, or quality has very little strength or intensity.

★ **starve** [staːrv] v. 굶주리다, 굶어죽다
If you are starving, you feel very hungry.

복습 **glow** [glou] v. 빛나다, 타다; (얼굴이) 상기되다; n. (은은한) 불빛; 홍조
If something glows, it produces a dull, steady light.

복습 **brick** [brik] n. 벽돌
Bricks are rectangular blocks of baked clay used for building walls, which are usually red or brown.

복습 **wave** [weiv] v. (손·팔을) 흔들다; 흔들리다; n. (손·팔을) 흔들기; 파도, 물결
If you wave or wave your hand, you move your hand from side to side in the air, usually in order to say hello or goodbye to someone.

★ **disappear** [disəpíər] v. 사라지다, 보이지 않게 되다; 없어지다; 실종되다
If you say that someone or something disappears, you mean that you can no longer see them, usually because you or they have changed position.

★ **sideways** [sáidwèiz] ad. 옆으로; 옆에서
Sideways means in a direction to the left or right, not forward or backward.

복습 **hay** [hei] n. 건초
Hay is grass which has been cut and dried so that it can be used to feed animals.

복습 **never mind** idiom 신경쓰지 마, 괜찮아
You use 'never mind' to tell someone that they need not do something or worry about something, because it is not important or because you will do it yourself.

복습 **dear** [diər] n. 얘야; 여보, 당신; int. 이런!; 맙소사!; a. 사랑하는; ~에게
You can call someone dear as a sign of affection.

★ **click** [klik] v. 딸깍 하는 소리를 내다; n. 딸칵 (하는 소리)
If something clicks or if you click it, it makes a short, sharp sound.

edge [edʒ] v. 조금씩 움직이다; 테두리를 두르다; n. 끝, 가장자리; 우위
If someone or something edges somewhere, they move very slowly in that direction.

difficulty [dífikʌlti] n. 어려움, 곤경, 장애
A difficulty is a problem.

narrow [nǽrou] v. 좁아지다; a. 좁은
If something narrows, it becomes less wide.

scrape [skreip] v. (무엇을) 긁어내다; (상처가 나도록) 긁다; n. 긁기; 긁힌 상처
If something scrapes against something else or if someone or something scrapes something else, it rubs against it, making a noise or causing slight damage.

loosen [lu:sn] v. 느슨하게 하다; 풀다; (통제·구속 등을) 완화하다
If you loosen your clothing or something that is tied or fastened or if it loosens, you undo it slightly so that it is less tight or less firmly held in place.

press [pres] v. 누르다; 밀다; (무엇에) 바짝 대다; n. 언론; 인쇄
If you press something or press down on it, you push hard against it with your foot or hand.

wiggle [wigl] v. 꿈틀꿈틀 움직이다; n. 꿈틀꿈틀 움직이기
If you wiggle something or if it wiggles, it moves up and down or from side to side in small quick movements.

dead end [ded énd] n. 막다른 길; 막다른 지경
If a street is a dead end, there is no way out at one end of it.

swing [swiŋ] n. 흔들기; 휘두르기; v. (swung–swung) (전후·좌우로) 흔들다; 휙 움직이다
Swing is movement in alternate directions or in a particular direction.

branch [brænʧ] v. 갈라지다, 나뉘다; n. 나뭇가지; 지사, 분점
If something branches, it divides into two or more parts.

widen [waidn] v. 넓어지다; (정도·범위 등이) 커지다

If you widen something or if it widens, it becomes greater in measurement from one side or edge to the other.

blah [blaː] int. 어쩌고저쩌고

You use 'blah, blah, blah' to refer to something that is said or written without giving the actual words, because you think that they are boring or unimportant.

★ **cave** [keiv] n. 동굴

A cave is a large hole in the side of a cliff or hill, or one that is under the ground.

smudge [smʌdʒ] v. 더럽히다, 더러워지다; n. (더러운) 자국, 얼룩

If you smudge a surface, you make it dirty by touching it and leaving a substance on it.

★ **dirt** [dəːrt] n. 흙; 먼지, 때

You can refer to the earth on the ground as dirt, especially when it is dusty.

squint [skwint] v. 눈을 가늘게 뜨고 보다; 사시이다; n. 사시; 잠깐 봄

If you squint at something, you look at it with your eyes partly closed.

exclaim [ikskléim] v. 소리치다, 외치다

If you exclaim, you cry out suddenly in surprise, strong emotion, or pain.

★ **temper** [témpər] n. (화를 내는) 성질; 기분; v. 누그러뜨리다, 완화시키다
(lose one's temper idiom 화를 내다)

If you lose your temper, you become so angry that you shout at someone or show in some other way that you are no longer in control of yourself.

roll one's eyes idiom 눈을 굴리다

If you roll your eyes, they move round and upward. People sometimes roll their eyes when they are frightened, bored, or annoyed.

bite [bait] n. 한 입; 물기; v. (이빨로) 물다; 베어 물다

A bite of something, especially food, is the action of biting it.

* **sip** [sip] v. (음료를) 홀짝거리다, 조금씩 마시다; n. 한 모금
If you sip a drink or sip at it, you drink by taking just a small amount at a time.

* **jerk** [dʒəːrk] v. 홱 움직이다; n. 홱 움직임; 얼간이
If you jerk something or someone in a particular direction, or they jerk in a particular direction, they move a short distance very suddenly and quickly.

* **thumb** [θʌm] n. 엄지손가락; v. 엄지손가락으로 건드리다
Your thumb is the short thick part on the side of your hand next to your four fingers.

* **cheer** [tʃiər] v. 환호하다; 응원하다, 힘을 북돋우다; n. 환호 (cheering n. 환호)
When people cheer, they shout loudly to show their approval or to encourage someone who is doing something such as taking part in a game.

* **mess** [mes] n. 엉망인 상황; (지저분하고) 엉망인 상태; v. 엉망으로 만들다
If you say that a situation is a mess, you mean that it is full of trouble or problems.

* **sign** [sain] n. 표지판, 간판; 징후; 몸짓; v. 서명하다; 신호를 보내다
A sign is a piece of wood, metal, or plastic with words or pictures on it. Signs give you information about something, or give you a warning or an instruction.

keep out idiom (~에) 들어가지 마라
'Keep out' is used on signs to tell people not to go into a place.

parking lot [páːrkiŋ lat] n. 주차장
A parking lot is an area of ground where people can leave their cars.

* **barely** [bέərli] ad. 간신히, 가까스로; 거의 ~아니게
You use barely to say that something is only just true or only just the case.

복습 **squeeze** [skwi:z] v. (좁은 곳에) 비집고 들어가다; (꼭) 쥐다; n. (손으로 꼭) 쥐기
If you squeeze a person or thing somewhere or if they squeeze there, they manage to get through or into a small space.

interrupt [ìntərʌ́pt] v. (말·행동을) 방해하다; 중단시키다; 차단하다
If you interrupt someone who is speaking, you say or do something that causes them to stop.

rest [rest] n. 나머지; 휴식; v. 쉬다; 놓이다, (~에) 있다
The rest is used to refer to all the parts of something or all the things in a group that remain or that you have not already mentioned.

crash [kræʃ] v. 박살나다; 충돌하다; 굉음을 내다; n. (자동차·항공기) 사고; 요란한 소리
(crash down idiom 부서지다, 붕괴하다)
If a building or a wall crashes down, it falls with a very loud noise.

go on idiom (어떤 상황이) 계속되다; 말을 계속하다
To go on means to continue to happen or exist without changing.

solid [sálid] a. 단단한; 견고한; 고체의; n. 고체, 고형물
A substance that is solid is very hard or firm.

splinter [splíntər] v. 쪼개지다, 깨지다; 분열되다; n. (나무·금속·유리 등의) 조각
If something splinters or is splintered, it breaks into thin, sharp pieces.

board [bɔːrd] n. 판자; 이사회; v. 승선하다, 탑승하다
A board is a flat, thin, rectangular piece of wood or plastic which is used for a particular purpose.

bit [bit] n. 조금, 약간; 조각; 부분, 일부
A bit means to a small extent or degree.

jagged [dʒǽgid] a. 삐죽삐죽한, 들쭉날쭉한
Something that is jagged has a rough, uneven shape or edge with lots of sharp points.

protrude [proutrú:d] v. 튀어나오다, 돌출되다
If something protrudes from somewhere, it sticks out.

waist [weist] n. 허리
Your waist is the middle part of your body where it narrows slightly above your hips.

tug [tʌg] v. (세게) 잡아당기다; n. (갑자기 세게) 잡아당김
If you tug something or tug at it, you give it a quick and usually strong pull.

loose [luːs] a. (흙 등이) 단단하지 않은; 헐거워진, 풀린; v. 느슨하게 하다
If something is loose in texture, there is space between the different particles or threads it consists of.

poke [pouk] v. (손가락 등으로) 쿡 찌르다; 쑥 내밀다; n. (손가락 등으로) 찌르기
If you poke someone or something, you quickly push them with your finger or with a sharp object.

stick [stik] n. 막대기, 나무토막; v. 찌르다, 박다; 붙이다, 붙다
A stick is a long thin piece of wood which is used for a particular purpose.

cascade [kæskéid] v. 폭포처럼 흐르다; 풍성하게 늘어지다; n. 폭포처럼 쏟아지는 물
To cascade means to flow down or hang down in large amounts.

cover [kʌ́vər] v. 덮다; 씌우다, 가리다; n. 몸을 숨길 곳; 덮개
If one thing covers another, it forms a layer over its surface.

daylight [déilait] n. (낮의) 햇빛, 일광
Daylight is the natural light that there is during the day, before it gets dark.

unmistakable [ʌ̀nmistéikəbl] a. 오해의 여지가 없는, 틀림없는
(unmistakably ad. 틀림없이, 명백하게)
If you describe something as unmistakable, you mean that it is so obvious that it cannot be mistaken for anything else.

bottom [bátəm] n. 맨 아래 (부분); 바닥; (아래쪽) 뒷면
The bottom of something is the lowest or deepest part of it.

✫ **limit** [límit] v. 제한하다; 한정하다; n. 한계, 한도; 제한

If you limit something, you prevent it from becoming greater than a particular amount or degree.

복습 **opening** [óupəniŋ] n. 구멍, 틈; 시작

An opening is a hole or empty space through which things or people can pass.

✦ **courtyard** [kɔ́:rtjà:rd] n. 안뜰, 안마당

A courtyard is an open area of ground which is surrounded by buildings or walls.

복습 **get it** idiom 이해하다; 야단맞다, 벌받다

To get it means to understand an argument or the person making it.

✦ **yell** [jel] v. 고함치다, 소리 지르다; n. 고함, 외침

If you yell, you shout loudly, usually because you are excited, angry, or in pain.

✫ **crawl** [krɔ:l] v. (엎드려) 기다; 몹시 느리게 가다; n. 기어가기; 서행

When you crawl, you move forward on your hands and knees.

Hero!

1. How did Emma feel while the pictures were being taken?

  A. She still didn't consider Stanley to be a hero.

  B. She was proud to be standing next to Stanley.

  C. She was shy about having her picture taken.

  D. She didn't want Flash Tobin to take any pictures of her.

2. What did Chief Johnson say about Stanley suddenly becoming round again?

  A. It was not as interesting as he had expected.

  B. It was something he had never seen before.

  C. It was great that Stanley was normal again.

  D. It was too bad that Stanley was no longer flat.

3. **What caused Stanley to become round again?**
   A. The kiss from Mrs. Lambchop and the poke from Emma
   B. The kiss from Mrs. Lambchop and the handshake with Chief
   Johnson
   C. The handshake with Chief Johnson and the slap on the back
   from Flash Tobin
   D. The slap on the back from Flash Tobin and the poke from
   Emma

4. **Why did everyone move away from the courtyard?**
   A. The courtyard was breaking apart.
   B. The courtyard was too small to fit everyone.
   C. The courtyard was too close to the Merker building.
   D. The courtyard was not the prettiest place to take pictures.

5. **What happened after the rest of the building came crashing down?**
   A. Emma realized that Stanley really had saved her.
   B. Emma admitted that she liked Stanley a lot.
   C. Everyone felt a bit sad that the building was ruined.
   D. Everyone panicked and ran away.

Check Your Reading Speed

1분에 몇 단어를 읽는지 리딩 속도를 측정해보세요.

$$\frac{445 \text{ words}}{\text{reading time (} \quad \text{) sec}} \times 60 = (\quad) \text{ WPM}$$

Build Your Vocabulary

rejoice [ridʒɔ́is] v. 크게 기뻐하다

If you rejoice, you are very pleased about something and you show it in your behavior.

courtyard [kɔ́:rtjà:rd] n. 안뜰, 안마당

A courtyard is an open area of ground which is surrounded by buildings or walls.

chief [ʧi:f] n. (조직·집단의) 장(長); a. (계급·직급상) 최고위자인

The chief of an organization is the person who is in charge of it.

announce [ənáuns] v. 발표하다, 알리다; 선언하다

If you announce something, you tell people about it publicly or officially.

exact [igzǽkt] a. 정확한, 정밀한; 꼼꼼한, 빈틈없는 (exactly ad. 정확히, 꼭, 틀림없이)

You use exactly before an amount, number, or position to emphasize that it is no more, no less, or no different from what you are stating.

cheerful [ʧíərfəl] a. 발랄한, 쾌활한; 쾌적한

Something that is cheerful is pleasant and makes you feel happy.

slap [slæp] n. 철썩 때리기, 치기; v. (손바닥으로) 철썩 때리다; 털썩 놓다

A slap is a sharp hit with the palm of the hand.

elbow [élbou] n. 팔꿈치; v. (팔꿈치로) 밀치다

Your elbow is the part of your arm where the upper and lower halves of the arm are joined.

80

jab [dʒæb] v. (쿡) 찌르다; n. (쿡) 찌르기; (권투에서) 잽
If you jab one thing into another, you push it there with a quick, sudden movement and with a lot of force.

rib [rib] n. 갈비(뼈), 늑골
Your ribs are the 12 pairs of curved bones that surround your chest.

yell [jel] v. 고함치다, 소리 지르다; n. 고함, 외침
If you yell, you shout loudly, usually because you are excited, angry, or in pain.

grin [grin] v. 활짝 웃다; n. 활짝 웃음
When you grin, you smile broadly.

stare [stɛər] v. 빤히 쳐다보다, 응시하다; n. 빤히 쳐다보기, 응시
If you stare at someone or something, you look at them for a long time.

peculiar [pikjúːljər] a. 기묘한, 이상한; 특유한, 고유의
If you describe someone or something as peculiar, you think that they are strange or unusual, sometimes in an unpleasant way.

hooray [huréi] int. 만세
People sometimes shout 'hooray!' when they are very happy and excited about something.

aim [eim] v. 겨누다; 목표하다; n. 겨냥, 조준; 목적
If you aim a weapon or object at something or someone, you point it toward them before firing or throwing it.

hold it idiom 기다려
You can use 'Hold it' to tell someone to wait a moment.

regular [régjulər] a. 일반적인, 평범한; 규칙적인
Regular is used to mean 'normal.'

applaud [əplɔ́ːd] v. 박수를 치다; 갈채를 보내다
When a group of people applaud, they clap their hands in order to show approval, for example when they have enjoyed a play or concert.

department [dipá:rtmənt] n. 부서 (fire department n. 소방국)
The fire department is an organization which has the job of putting out fires.

osteal [ástiəl] a. (= osseous) 뼈로 이루어진; 뼈가 된
Oteal means of or relating to bone or to the skeleton.

poke [pouk] n. (손가락 등으로) 찌르기; v. (손가락 등으로) 쿡 찌르다; 쑥 내밀다
A poke is a quick push with your finger or a pointed object.

board [bɔ:rd] n. 판자; 이사회; v. 승선하다, 탑승하다
A board is a flat, thin, rectangular piece of wood or plastic which is used for a particular purpose.

tilt [tilt] v. 기울다, (뒤로) 젖혀지다; n. 기울어짐, 젖혀짐
If you tilt an object or if it tilts, it moves into a sloping position with one end or side higher than the other.

roof [ru:f] n. 지붕; v. 지붕을 씌우다
The roof of a building is the covering on top of it that protects the people and things inside from the weather.

land [lænd] v. (땅에) 떨어지다; (땅·표면에) 내려앉다, 착륙하다; n. 육지, 땅; 지역
When someone or something lands, they come down to the ground after moving through the air or falling.

folk [fouk] n. (pl.) 여러분, 얘들아; (pl.) (일반적인) 사람들; (pl.) 부모
You can use folks as a term of address when you are talking to several people.

creak [kri:k] v. 삐걱거리다; n. 삐걱거리는 소리
If something creaks, it makes a short, high-pitched sound when it moves.

grind [graind] v. 삐걱거리다; 갈다; 비비다; n. 삐걱거리는 소리
When something grinds, it rubs against something else making a harsh, unpleasant sound.

crash [kræʃ] v. 박살나다; 충돌하다; 굉음을 내다; n. (자동차·항공기) 사고; 요란한 소리
(crash down idiom 부서지다, 붕괴하다)
If a building or a wall crashes down, it falls with a very loud noise.

catch one's eye idiom 눈길을 끌다; 눈에 띄다
If you catch someone's eye, you do something to attract their attention,
so that you can speak to them.

nod [nad] n. (고개를) 끄덕임; v. (고개를) 끄덕이다, 까딱하다
A nod is a movement up and down with the head.

puzzle [pʌzl] v. 어리둥절하게 하다; n. 퍼즐; 수수께끼
(puzzled a. 어리둥절해하는, 얼떨떨한)
Someone who is puzzled is confused because they do not understand
something.

cheek [ʧiːk] n. 뺨, 볼; 엉덩이
Your cheeks are the sides of your face below your eyes.

Fame!

1. What did the Lambchops do in the evening?

    A. They read the newspaper for the first time that day.

    B. They watched the news on TV for the first time that day.

    C. They read the newspaper for the second time that day.

    D. They watched the news on TV for the second time that day.

2. What did Arthur think of the family picture?

    A. He thought everyone in the picture looked cheerful.

    B. He thought the picture was too small.

    C. He was happy to finally see a picture with him in it.

    D. He was pleased with how big the picture was.

3. **How did Stanley feel about the pictures?**

   A. He was completely embarrassed by them.

   B. He wasn't particularly interested in them.

   C. He wanted to keep both of them.

   D. He liked the picture with Emma most.

4. **What did Dr. Dan say to Mrs. Lambchop about Stanley becoming flat in the future?**

   A. It would probably not happen again.

   B. It could never happen again.

   C. It would definitely happen again.

   D. There was a strong possibility that it could happen again.

5. **What did Arthur do with the family picture?**

   A. He wrote "My Brother" in the white space at the bottom.

   B. He drew an arrow pointing to Stanley.

   C. He taped the picture to the kitchen wall.

   D. He put the picture above his bed.

Check Your Reading Speed

1분에 몇 단어를 읽는지 리딩 속도를 측정해보세요.

$$\frac{204 \text{ words}}{\text{reading time (\quad) sec}} \times 60 = (\qquad) \text{ WPM}$$

Build Your Vocabulary

⭑ **fame** [feim] n. 명성
If you achieve fame, you become very well-known.

복습 **bedtime** [bédtàim] n. 취침 시간, 잠자리에 드는 시간
Your bedtime is the time when you usually go to bed.

⭑ **headline** [hédlain] n. (신문 기사의) 표제; v. (기사에) 표제를 달다
A headline is the title of a newspaper story, printed in large letters at the top of the story, especially on the front page.

복습 **rescue** [réskju:] v. 구하다, 구출하다; n. 구출, 구조, 구제 (rescuer n. 구조자, 구출자)
If you rescue someone, you get them out of a dangerous or unpleasant situation.

복습 **regain** [rigéin] v. 되찾다, 회복하다; 되돌아오다
If you regain something that you have lost, you get it back again.

⭑ **beneath** [biní:θ] prep. 아래에
Something that is beneath another thing is under the other thing.

복습 **poke** [pouk] v. (손가락 등으로) 쿡 찌르다; 쑥 내밀다; n. (손가락 등으로) 찌르기
If you poke someone or something, you quickly push them with your finger or with a sharp object.

복습 **rib** [rib] n. 갈비(뼈), 늑골
Your ribs are the 12 pairs of curved bones that surround your chest.

86

particular [pərtíkjulər] a. 특정한; 특별한; 까다로운 (particularly ad. 특히, 특별히)
Particularly means more than usual or more than other things.

pleased [pli:zd] a. 기쁜, 기뻐하는, 만족해하는
If you are pleased, you are happy about something or satisfied with something.

pat [pæt] v. 쓰다듬다; 가볍게 두드리다; n. 쓰다듬기, 토닥거리기
If you pat something or someone, you tap them lightly, usually with your hand held flat.

recover [rikʌvər] v. (의식 등을) 되찾다; 회복되다; (손실 등을) 되찾다
(recovery n. (건강) 회복)
You talk about the recovery of someone's physical or mental state when they return to this state.

dear [diər] n. 얘야; 여보, 당신; int. 이런!; 맙소사!; a. 사랑하는; ~에게
You can call someone dear as a sign of affection.

unlikely [ʌnláikli] a. 있음직하지 않은; 예상 밖의
If you say that something is unlikely to happen or unlikely to be true, you believe that it will not happen or that it is not true, although you are not completely sure.

occur [əkə́:r] v. 일어나다, 발생하다; (어디에) 존재하다
When something occurs, it happens.

arrow [ǽrou] n. 화살표; 화살
An arrow is a written or printed sign that consists of a straight line with another line bent at a sharp angle at one end.

bottom [bátəm] n. 맨 아래 (부분); 바닥; (아래쪽) 뒷면
The bottom of something is the lowest or deepest part of it.

tape [teip] v. 테이프로 붙이다; 끈으로 묶다; 녹음하다; n. (접착용) 테이프
If you tape one thing to another, you attach it using sticky tape.

1장 아침에 일어난 놀라운 일

램찹 부인(Mrs. Lambchop)이 아침 식사를 준비하고 있었습니다. 램찹 씨(Mr. Lambchop)는, 부엌 식탁에서, 아침 신문의 일부를 읽으면서 돕고 있었습니다.

"여기에 이상한 기사가 실렸어요, 해리엇(Harriet)." 그가 말했습니다. "스웨덴에 자전거를 타는 닭이 있대요."

"나도 탈 수 있어요, 조지(George)." 제대로 듣지 않으면서, 램찹 부인이 말했습니다.

"이것 좀 들어 봐요. '비워진 머커 건물. 다음 주에 허물 예정.' 상상해 봐요! 팔 층 건물이잖아요!"

"참 안됐네요!" 램찹 부인이 접시들을 놓았습니다. "얘들아!" 그녀가 불렀습니다. "아침이 준비됐단다!"

그녀의 시선이 개수대 위 벽에 줄지어 걸린 사진들에 닿았습니다. 밤사이에 침실 벽에 걸린 큰 게시판이 몸 위로 떨어지면서, 고작 반 인치(1.27센티미터)의 두께가 되어버린, 미소 짓는 스탠리(Stanley)의 사진이 있었습니다. 다음으로는 스탠리의 남동생, 아서(Arthur)가 재치 있게 자전거 공기 주입 펌프로 그를 불어 다시 둥그렇게 만든 이후에 일어났던 많은 가족 모험을 떠올리게 하는 사진들이 있었습니다. 우연히 스탠리에 의해 램프 밖으로 불려 나온 뒤 그들 모두를 위해 소원을 들어주었던 어린 요정(genie), 하라즈 왕자(Prince Haraz)와 함께 있는 형제의 사진이 있었습니다. 크리스마스 때 북극에 방문해서 산타클로스와 그의 딸, 사라(Sarah)와 온 가족이 함께 찍은 사진도 있었습니다. 그들에게 우주로 가는 기밀 임무를 수행해달라고 부탁했던, 미국 대통령의 워싱턴 D.C. 집무실에 있는 가족의 사진도 있었습니다. 마지막 사진은 램찹 부인이 스탠리의 얼굴 그림을 위에 그린 풍선 옆에 서 있는 아서의 모습을 보여주었습니다. 사실 스탠리가 끈을 잡고 있는, 그 풍선은, 그가 있다는 것을 알리는 귀중한 지표였는데, 당시에 그가 눈에 보이지 않았기 때문입니다. "얘들아!" 그녀가 다시 불렀습니다. "아침 먹어라!"

그들의 침실에서, 스탠리와 아서는 마저 옷을 입고 있었습니다.

스탠리가 자신의 가방을 싸는 동안, 아서는 테니스공을 튕겼습니다. "가자." 그가 말했습니다. "여기! 잡아 봐!"

스탠리는 막 자기 침대 옆 선반 위에 있는 책으로 손을 뻗었습니다. 그가 돌아설 때 공이 그의 등을 때렸고, 그는 선반 모서리에 자기 어깨를 쿵 하고 부딪혔습니다.

"아야!"

"미안해." 아서가 말했습니다. "그런데 어서 가자, 응? 형도 알잖아, 얼마나 오래—스탠리 형!"

"왜 소리 지르고 그래?" 스탠리가 자기 가방을 고쳐 매었습니다. "서둘러! 나 정말 배고프—" 그가 말을 멈췄습니다. "오, 맙소사! 아서, 너도 보이지?"

"실은, 나도 보여." 아서가 크게 침을 삼켰습니다. "형은, 있지 . . . 납작해졌어."

형제는 서로를 쳐다보았습니다.

"펌프는?" 스탠리가 말했습니다. "그게 또 통할지도 몰라."

아서가 그들의 장난감 상자에서 자전거 공기 주입 펌프를 가져왔고, 스탠리는 그의 침대 위에 누워서 호스 끝을 자신의 입으로 물었습니다.

아서는 길고, 규칙적으로 펌프질했습니다.

스탠리가 인상을 찌푸렸습니다. "그거 아파!"

아서가 다시 펌프질했고, 스탠리가 자기 입에서 호스를 홱 빼냈습니다. "아오오! 그거 정말 아프다고! 전이랑 달라. 우리 그만두는 게 좋겠어."

"이제 어떡하지?" 아서가 말했습니다. "우리가 그냥 이곳에 영원히 숨어있을 수는 없잖아, 형도 알겠지만."

램찹 부인이 부르는 소리가 다시 들렸습니다. "얘들아! 어서 오렴!"

"하나 부탁할게." 스탠리가 말했습니다. "네가 가서 부모님께 말해 줘. 부모님께서 대비할 수 있게 하는 거야, 알겠지?"

"알았어." 아서가 말했고, 이야기하러 갔습니다.

* * *

아서가 부엌 문가에 서 있었습니다. "있잖아요(hey), 맞춰 보실래요?" 그가 말했습니다.

"건초(hay)는 말을 위한 거란다, 얘야." 램찹 부인이 말했습니다. "좋은 아침이구나! 아침 식사가 준비되었단다."

"안녕, 아서." 램찹 씨가 자신의 신문 뒤에서 말했습니다. "스탠리는 어디에 있니?"

"맞춰 보실래요?" 아서가 다시 말했습니다.

램찹 부인이 한숨 쉬었습니다. "그래, 좋아! 난 맞추지 못하겠구나. 말해 주렴."

"스탠리 형이 다시 납작해졌어요." 아서가 말했습니다.

램찹 씨는 그의 신문을 내려놓았습니다.

램찹 부인은 자신의 두 눈을 감았습니다. "다시 납작해졌다고? 너 그렇게 말한 거니?"

"네." 아서가 말했습니다.

"정말이에요." 스탠리는 이제 아서 옆

문가에 서 있었습니다. "좀 보세요."

"세상에 맙소사!" 램찹 씨가 말했습니다. "난 믿을 수가 없어, 그 게시판이—"

"그건 이번에 제 위로 떨어지지 않았어요." 스탠리가 말했습니다. "전 그냥 납작해져 버렸어요. 아서가 전에 했던 것처럼, 제게 공기를 넣으려고 했는데, 너무 아팠어요."

"오, 스탠리!" 램찹 부인이 달려가서 그에게 키스해 주었습니다. "너 지금 기분이 어떠니?"

"사실, 괜찮아요." 스탠리가 말했습니다. "그냥 놀랐을 뿐이에요. 저 학교에 가도 되나요?"

램찹 부인이 잠시 생각했습니다. "좋아. 아침을 먹으렴. 학교가 끝난 뒤에 댄 의사 선생님(Dr. Dan)이 뭐라고 말할지 들어 보자."

2장 댄 의사 선생님

"아, 램찹 씨 그리고 램찹 부인! 그리고 얘들아!" 그들이 그의 진료실로 들어오자 댄 선생님이 말했습니다. "성말 반갑네요—"

그의 두 눈이 휘둥그레졌습니다. "이럴 수가, 스탠리! 램찹 씨, 당신은 정말로 그 게시판에 대해 뭔가를 해야겠어요!"

"그건 여전히 제자리에 단단히 붙어 있어요, 댄 선생님." 램찹 부인이 말했습니다. "우리는 이번에 납작해지는 병에 걸린 것에 대해 어떻게 설명해야 할지 모르겠어요."

"흠." 댄 선생님이 잠시 생각했습니다. "혹시, 납작해지는 병에 걸리는 가족력이 있나요?"

"아니요." 램찹 씨가 말했습니다. "그렇다면 우리가 기억했을 거예요."

"우리는 학교에 가려고 옷을 입고 있었어요." 스탠리가 설명했습니다. "우리는 심지어 아침을 먹지도 않았어요. 그리고 갑자기, 제가 납작해졌어요."

댄 선생님이 얼굴을 찌푸렸습니다. "아무 일도 일어나지 않았다고? 전혀 아무 일도 말이니?"

"뭐, 아서가 절 테니스공으로 때렸어요." 스탠리가 말했습니다. "그리고 나서 전 제 어깨를 부딪쳤는데—"

"아하!" 벌떡 일어나서, 댄 선생님이 그의 책상 뒤에 있는 책꽂이에서 커다란 책을 꺼냈고 책장을 넘기기 시작했습니다. "이건 프란츠 게마이스터 박사 (Dr. Franz Gemeister)가 쓴 어렵고 득이한 사례들이라는 훌륭한 책이에요. 제가 찾기만 하면 . . . 여기 있네요! '납작해짐, 217쪽!'"

그가 큰소리로 읽었습니다. "'갑작스러운 납작해짐 . . . 매우 드물며 . . .

아주 적은 기록만 있음 . . . 전해 들은 이야기들 . . .' 아, 여기 있네요! 5세기경으로 거슬러 올라가요! '전투 중에, 사나운 몽고(Mongo the Fierce)라는, 훈족(the Hun)의 아틸라 왕(Attila)의 부관이 동시에, 두 번, 뒤에서 맞았는데, 즉시 그의 방패 정도의 두께로 변했다. 그는 금속판 몽고라고 알려지게 되었고, 그의 원래 둘레를 되찾지 못한 채 오랫동안 살았다.'"

댄 선생님이 책을 덮었습니다. "제가 생각하던 대로입니다! OBP예요."

"뭐라고요?" 램찹 부인이 말했습니다.

"OBP. 뼈 균형점(Osteal Balance Point)입니다." 댄 선생님이 설명했습니다. "잘 알려지지 않은 해부학적 특징이지요. 인간의 몸은, 물론, 복잡한 기적 같은 것으로, 그 뼈대는 지지와 균형으로 이루어진 섬세한 골격이죠. 뼈 균형점은 상체의 거의 어느 곳에서나 존재할 수 있어요. 나이 그리고 연관된 개인이 가진, 말하자면, 특정한 '의도'에 따라서 달라지는 두 지점에 동시에 가해지는 압박에만 취약합니다. 제 소견으로는, 테니스공과 선반 모서리로 인해 일어난 압박이 스탠리의 OBP에 영향을 주었고, 그것 때문에 그를 납작하게 한 것 같습니다."

잠시, 모든 사람이 침묵했습니다.

"처음 스탠리가 납작해졌을 때, 선생님은 그의 상태에 대해 굉장히 당혹스러워했지요." 마침내 램찹 씨가 말했습니다. "지금은 선생님이 놀라울 정도로 잘 알고 있는 것처럼 보이네요."

"전 그에 대해 많이 공부했지요." 댄 선생님이 말했습니다.

램찹 부인이 한숨 쉬었습니다. "아마도 우리는 다른 의견을 구하는 게 좋겠어요. OBP에 대해 누가 세계에서 제일 뛰어난 권위자인가요?"

"그건 저일 겁니다." 댄 선생님이 말했습니다.

"그렇군요. . . . 흠, 우리는 선생님의 시간을 충분히 빼앗은 것 같네요." 램찹 씨가 일어나며, 자신의 가족에게 따라오라고 손짓했습니다. "고맙습니다, 댄 선생님."

문에서, 램찹 부인이 돌아섰습니다. "혹시 만약에 우리가, 있잖아요, OBP를 찾게 된다면, 우리가 스탠리를—"

"아니, 안 됩니다!" 댄 선생님이 말했습니다. "이 녀석에게 그런 골격의 압박을 또 겪게 하는 건 위험할 거예요! 그리고 OBP를 찾는다고요? 유감스럽지만, 그럴 확률이 희박할 겁니다."

아서에게 아이디어가 떠올랐습니다. "알아냈어요! 만약 우리가 모두 막대기를 들고 동시에 스탠리 형의 온몸을 때리고, 계속 그런다면, 그럼—"

"그 정도면 됐구나, 아서." 램찹 씨가 말했고, 자신의 가족을 데리고 나갔습니다.

3장 스탠리 항해하다

다음 주 일요일 이른 아침에, 램찹 씨는 오랜 대학 친구, 랠프 존스(Ralph Jones)에게서 전화를 받았습니다.

"단지 너에게 상기시켜 주고 싶었어, 조지, 스탠리와 내가 오늘 항해를 하러 가기로 약속했다는 걸 말이야." 그가 말했습니다.

"그도 그 일을 기대하고 있어, 랠프." 램찹 씨가 망설였습니다. "아마도, 내가 말해야만 할 것 같은데, 스탠리가 다시 납작해졌다는 사실을 말이야."

존스 씨가 한숨을 쉬었습니다. "난 그가 그 일을 극복했다고 생각했는데. 흠, 내가 그를 10시에 데리러 갈게."

그날 아침 늦게, 스탠리와 함께 해변에 있는 그의 항해 클럽으로 차를 타고 가면서, 존스 씨는 자신이 한 번 램찹 가족과 함께 만난 적이 있는 외국에서 온 손님에 대해 물었습니다. "왕자였지, 응? 그를 최근에도 봤었니?"

스탠리는 그가 어린 요정, 하라즈 왕자를 가리킨다는 것을 알았지만, 요정에 대한 이야기도 그렇고, 하라즈가 그

가 떠나왔었던 요정 나라로 돌아갔다는 것을 설명하기 어려웠습니다.

"아니요." 스탠리가 말했습니다. "사실, 그는 집으로 갔어요."

"아쉽구나." 존스 씨는 그의 놀라운 기억력으로 유명했습니다. "내가 기억하기로는, 하라즈였어. 파우지 무스타파 아슬란 미르자 멜렉 나머드 하라즈 왕자(Prince Fawzi Mustafa Aslan Mirza Melek Namerd Haraz)였지?"

"맞아요." 스탠리가 말했습니다.

항해 클럽이 있는 부두에서, 존스 씨는 자신의 배, 러브버그(*Lovebug*)를 준비했고, 그걸 스탠리에게 설명해 주었습니다. "여기 있는 이 큰 돛은 주범(mainsail)이고, 저기 뒤에 있는 저건 배의 키란다, 조종하는 데 필요하지. 이 지퍼가 달린 가방 안에는 다른 돛이 있는데, 스피나커(spinnaker)라고 부른단다. 우리가 순풍을 받으며 항해할 때 우리는 더 속도를 내려고 그걸 사용할 거야. 저 멀리 나가 있는 배를 보렴, 그것에 달린 스피나커가 어떻게 앞이 부풀어 올랐는지 말이야?"

스탠리가 웃있습니다. 스피나커는 옆으로 누워 있는 펼쳐진 우산처럼 보였습니다.

"저기 보이니." 존스 씨가 계속 말했습니다. "심판이 탄, 위원회 배와 빨간 부표 사이? 저게 출발선이야. 경주는

또 저기로 돌아오는 것으로 끝나지. 저 선을 지나는 첫 번째 배가 이기는 거란다!"

그는 계류용 밧줄을 풀어 던졌고, 주 범이바람을 받게 했습니다. *러브버그*는 다른 배들과 합류하려고 밖으로 나아갔습니다.

존스 씨가 가리켰습니다. "저기! 저건 재스퍼 그린(Jasper Green)의 배, *윈드스웹트(Windswept)*란다. 그는 내가 특히 이기고 싶은 사람이야!"

"왜요? 아저씨는 그 사람에게 화났어요?" 스탠리가 물었습니다.

"그는 언젠가 나에게 무척 무례하게 굴었단다. 하지만 신경 쓰지 말렴. 우리가 이길 수 있도록 확실히 준비하자!"

출발선 뒤에서, 그들은 자신들이 윈드스웹트 옆에 있다는 걸 알게 되었습니다. 재스퍼 그린이 친절하게 손을 흔들었지만, 랠프 존스는 그를 무시했습니다.

"넌 나와 함께 있으면 항상 기분이 좋아 보이지 않네, 랠프." 그린 씨가 말했습니다. "왜 그러는 거야? 나는 모르겠―이제 출발이야!"

총이 발포되면서 경주의 시작을 알렸습니다. *러브버그*와 *윈드스웹트* 그리고 다른 경주에 참여한 배들이 선명한 초록색 장식 테이프가 달린 부표로 표시된 경로를 따라 그들을 이끄는, 위원회의 모터보트 뒤에서 출발선을 지나 미끄러지듯 나아갔습니다.

스탠리는 편안하게 앉아서, 즐거워했습니다. 해는 환하게 떴고, 그의 얼굴에 닿는 바람이 상쾌했으며, 하늘은 맑고 파랗고, 바다는 아름다운 청회색을 띠었습니다. 그들 양옆, 그리고 앞에도, 뒤에도 배가 있었습니다. 바람을 맞아 그것들의 하얀 돛이 부풀어 오르면서 탁탁거리는 경쾌한 소리를 내는, 배들이 정말 예뻤습니다!

해변을 따라, 사람들이 집의 현관에서 손을 흔들었고, 그들의 목소리가 바람에 희미하게 실려 왔습니다. "잘한다! . . . 멋져요, 선원들! . . . 그들 중 한 사람은, 납작하게 보이네요!" 스탠리는 그 장난치는 말이 친절한 의미라는 걸 알고서, 손을 흔들어 답했습니다.

*러브버그*는 다른 배들을 지나쳤지만, 앞서 있는 다른 배들이 여전히 많았습니다. 그리고 이제 그들은 윈드스웹트와 거의 나란히 가고 있었습니다.

스탠리는 재스퍼 그린이 자신의 스피나커를 끌어 올린 것을 보았고, 다른 배들도 또한, 그렇게 했다는 걸 알았습니다.

"난 널 이기고 말 거야, 랠프!" 재스퍼 그린이 외쳤습니다.

"우리는 이 지점에서 돌아갈 거란다, 스탠리! 그리고―지금이야!" 랠프 존스가 외쳤습니다. "재스퍼에게 순풍을 받으며 항해한다는 것이 진짜 무엇을 의미하는지 보여 주자!"

그는 자신의 스피나커를 마룻줄에 달았고 돛대 위로 끌어 올렸습니다. 휘—이—익! 스피나커가 부풀었고, 스탠리는 *러브버그*가 마치 보이지 않는 손으로 민 것처럼, 앞으로 휙 하고 나아가는 걸 느꼈습니다.

"자 간다!" 랠프 존스가 소리쳤습니다.

그들은 다섯 척의 배를 더 지나쳤고, 세 척을 더, 그리고 윈드스웹트를 지나쳤습니다! 그들은 이제 모든 사람보다 앞서 있었고, 결승선이 앞에 놓여 있었습니다!

"우리가 이길 거예요!" 스탠리가 외쳤습니다.

"그래!" 랠프 존스가 소리치며 답했습니다. "기다리기만 하면 돼, 재스퍼가—"

찌—이—익!

위에서 소리가 들렸습니다. 올려다보자, 그들은 스피나커의 윗부분이 찢어신 것을 보았습니다.

찌—이—이—이—익!

찢어진 부분이 아래로 선을 그으며 내려왔고, 이제는 스피나커가 완전히 쭉 찢어진 채, 바람에 헛되이 펄럭였습니다. *러브버그*가 느려졌습니다.

"젠장!" 존스 씨는 주범으로 최선을 다했습니다. "제길, 제길, 제길!"

윈드스웹트가 그들 뒤로 다가왔습니다. "참 운도 없네!" 재스퍼 그린이 외쳤습니다. "하, 하!"

"젠장!" 존스 씨가 한숨 쉬었습니다. "우리가 할 수 있는 일이 없구나, 스탠리. 그렇지 않는 한—이건 미친 생각일 수 있어, 하지만 . . . 스탠리, 혹시 네가 우리의 스피나커가 되어줄 수 있겠니?"

"뭐라고요?" 스탠리가 소리쳤습니다. "어떻게요?"

"좋은 질문이야." 존스 씨가 말했습니다. "어디 보자. . . . 우선, 가서 돛대를 붙잡으렴. 바로 그거야. 이제는 아마도—"

"죄송하지만." 스탠리가 말했습니다. "아저씨는 전에 이렇게 해 본 적이 있나요?"

"스탠리, 아무도 전에 이런 일을 한 적 없단다." 존스 씨가 깊게 숨을 들이마셨습니다. "좋아. 이제 몸을 돌려서 앞을 봐, 그리고 네 머리 위로 네 뒤에 있는 돛대를 잡아!"

스탠리는 시키는 대로 하면서, 자기 몸을 제자리에 유지하기 위해 자신의 두 발을 보트 양옆에 단단히 두었습니다. 바람이 뒤에서 그를 밀어, *러브버그*가 결승선으로 나아가게 했습니다.

"그래! 가슴을 앞으로! 엉덩이는 뒤

로!" 존스 씨가 외쳤습니다. "내가 이제까지 가졌던 최고의 스피나커야!" 잠시 뒤 그들은 윈드스웹트를 지나쳤고, 스탠리는 재스퍼 그린의 얼굴에 지어진 놀라운 기색을 보고 웃지 않을 수 없었습니다.

그러고 나서 그들은 결승선을 통과했습니다! *러브버그*가 우승했습니다!

클럽 회관에 돌아와서, 재스퍼 그린은 자신이 졌다는 것을 인정할 수 없었습니다. 납작한 사람을 돛으로 쓸 수 있다고? 자신은 전에 *그런* 일을 결코 본 적이 없었다고, 그가 말했고, 경주 위원회 사무실에 불평하러 갔습니다. 하지만 그는 곧 돌아와서 *러브버그*가 정말로 이겼다고 알려 주었습니다. 위원회가 그에게 보트 경기에 참여한 일원에게 바람이 부는 것을 막는 어떤 조항도 없다고 알려 주었다고, 그는 말했습니다.

"훌륭한 항해였어, 랠프!" 그가 말했습니다. "난 그것이 내가 이긴 경기라고 생각했다고, 정말이야!"

"고맙네, 재스퍼." 존스 씨가 말했지만, 스탠리는 그가 미소 짓지 않는 걸 알아차렸습니다.

재스퍼 그린도 역시 눈치챘습니다. "랠프, 넌 여전히 나에게 화가 나 있군." 그가 말했습니다. "하지만 *왜?*"

"네가 내 흰 바지에 커피를 쏟았잖아, 재스퍼." 랠프 존스가 말했습니다.

"그리고 내가 펄쩍 뛰었을 때 넌 그냥 웃고만 있었지."

"뭐라고?" 재스퍼 그린은 몹시 놀란 듯했습니다. "난 기억하지 못하겠는데—어디에서? 언제?"

"우리는 점심을 함께하고 있었지." 존스 씨가 말했습니다. "오래된 반더쿡 호텔(Vandercook Hotel)에서 말이야."

"반더쿡이라고? 그건 20년 전에 문을 닫았잖아!" 그린 씨가 손바닥으로 자기 이마를 찰싹 때렸습니다. "난 기억이 나는군! 그 점심은 20년 전에 일어난 일이야, 랠프!"

"21년 전이야, 정확하게는."

"알았어, 알았다고!" 그린 씨가 말했습니다. "내가 사과할게, 맙소사!"

랠프 존스가 따뜻하게 미소 지었습니다. "정말 괜찮아, 재스퍼." 그가 말했습니다. "그 일에 대해 더는 신경 쓰지 말라고."

4장 학교로 돌아가다

스탠리는 그가 예전에 납작해졌던 일을 여전히 기억하는, 자신의 같은 반 친구들이 이제 그것에 대해 큰 법석을 떨지 않아서 기뻤습니다. 대부분 그들은 유쾌한 관심만을 드러냈습니다. "기분은 괜찮니, 스탠(Stan)?" 그들이 말했고,

"날카로워 보인다, 친구야! 날카롭다고, 알겠어? 농담을 이해했니?" 단지 심술 궂은 엠마 윅스(Emma Weeks)만 불쾌하게 굴었습니다. "허! 잘난 척하는 인간이 또 왔네!" 엠마가 어느 날 말했지만, 스탠리는 듣지 못한 척했습니다.

그가 학교에 돌아온 지 일주일 후에 신문사에서, 이 독특하게 생긴 학생에 대해 알고서는, 사진기자를 보내 취재하게 했습니다. 그는 축구 경기장에서 연습하는 걸 지켜보고 있는 스탠리를 찾았습니다.

"플래시 토빈(Flash Tobin)이란다." 그가 말했습니다. "데일리 센티널(Daily Sentinel)에서 나왔지. 네가 그 납작한 아이지, 그렇지?"

스탠리는 그가 농담하는 게 분명하다고 생각했습니다. "어떻게 알았어요?" 그가 다시 농담하며, 말했습니다.

"내가 어떻게 알았냐니—" 사진기자가 웃었습니다. "오, 이해했단다! 얘야, 내가 네 사진을 찍어도 되겠니? 바로 여기 골대 옆에서?"

스탠리는 고개를 끄덕였고, 플래시 토빈이 그의 사진을 찍었습니다. "난 전에 이곳에 납작한 아이가 있다고 들었단다." 그가 말했습니다. "유명한 미술관에서 좀도둑을 잡는 걸 도왔다고 했지. 하지만 그 아이는, 내가 듣기로는 다시 둥그렇게 변했다던데."

"그게 저예요." 스탠리가 그에게 말했습니다.

"넌 왔다 갔다 하는구나, 응?" 사진기자는 감명받았습니다. "좋아, 이제 둥그렇게 변해 보렴. 나는 그것도 역시 사진을 찍고 싶구나."

"제가 원한다고 해서 그냥 할 수 있는 게 아니에요." 스탠리가 설명했습니다. "처음에는, 제 동생이 저를 불어야만 했어요. 자전거 공기 주입 펌프로요."

"훌륭한 사진이 되었을 텐데!" 플래시 토빈이 자신의 고개를 저었습니다. "뭐, 우리는 그냥 납작한 모습을 찍어야겠구나."

스탠리의 사진은 다음 날 아침 데일리 센티널에 실렸고, 아서는 자신의 질투를 숨길 수가 없었습니다. 스탠리 형은 항상 신문에 그의 사진이 실려요, 라고 그가 말했습니다. 사람들은 그의 동생 사진을 싣는 게 얼마나 흥미로울지 모르는 걸까요?

오후에는 축구팀 연습이 있었고, 그날은 바람이 불었습니다. 코치가 말하기를, 스탠리가 바람에 날리는 모습이 걱정스럽다고 했습니다. 아마도, 팀을 위해, 그는 실내 스포츠로 바꾸는 게 좋을 것이라고 말이에요.

스탠리는 축구를 좋아했고, 그가 코치가 말한 것에 대해 더 생각하면 할수록, 그는 더 슬퍼졌습니다.

그의 담임 선생님인 엘리엇 선생님 (Miss Elliott)은 그가 평소의 활발한 모습이 아니라는 걸 알아차렸습니다. "레드필드 선생님(Mr. Redfield)은, 새로 오신 생활 지도 교사인데, 어려움을 겪는 학생들에게 무척 도움이 된다고 하는구나." 그녀가 그에게 말했습니다. "내가 그에게 너를 위해 시간을 낼 수 있는지 물어볼게."

엘리엇 선생님은 점심시간 후에 그에게 다시 말했습니다. "운이 좋구나, 스탠리! 레드필드 선생님이 오늘 학교가 끝난 뒤에 바로 너를 볼 수 있단다!"

"들어오렴, 스탠리. 거기에 앉으렴!" 레드필드 선생님이 편안한 의자를 가리켰습니다.

스탠리가 앉았고, 레드필드 선생님은 자기 책상에 앉아 뒤로 기대었습니다. "자 그럼. . . . 넌 네가 이곳에서 말한 어떤 내용도 완전히 비밀로 유지된다는 걸 알고 있니? 난 누구에게도 말하지 않을 거란다."

스탠리는 다른 사람의 관심을 끌 만한 말을 자신이 할 수나 있을지 궁금했습니다.

"엘리엇 선생님이 나에게 이야기하기로는 네가 어려움을 겪는 듯해 보인다고 하더라." 레드필드 선생님이 자신의 목소리를 낮추었습니다. "무엇이 문제니?"

"저도 사실은, 잘 모르겠어요." 스탠리가 말했습니다.

레드필드 선생님이 메모장과 펜을 들었습니다. "자유롭게 이야기하렴. 네 머릿속에 떠오르는 건 아무거나 말이야. 최근에 특별한 일이 일어났니?"

"뭐, 전 납작해졌어요." 스탠리가 말했습니다.

레드필드 선생님이 자신의 메모장에 메모했습니다. "나도 그걸 알겠구나, 그래. 그게 너에게 어떤 기분이 들게 하니?"

스탠리가 잠시 생각했습니다. "납작하다고요."

"그렇구나." 레드필드 선생님이 고개를 끄덕였습니다. "이 납작해진 일이, 너에게 전에도 일어났다고, 나는 들었단다. 너 자신에게 그걸 인정하지는 않지만, 네가 그 일이 다시 일어나기를 원했을 수도 있지 않을까?"

"말도 안 돼요!" 스탠리가 단호하게 말했습니다. "처음에는, 한동안은 재미있기도 했어요. 연처럼 날고, 우편으로 캘리포니아에 보내지기도 하고, 그런 일들이 말이에요. 하지만 그리고 전, 알겠지만, 그 일이 지겨워졌어요. 그리고 이제 저는 축구팀에서 쫓겨날지도 몰라요."

레드필드 선생님이 다시 고개를 끄덕

였습니다. "넌 네 독특한 모습에서 지금 어떤 즐거움도 누리고 있지 않니?"

스탠리가 잠시 생각했습니다. "뭐, 가끔이요." 그가 돛이 되었던 일과 랠프 존스가 경주에서 이기도록 도와준 일에 대해 이야기했습니다.

레드필드 선생님은 또 메모했습니다. "알겠구나. 돛이 되었다는 그 꿈 말이야, 넌 전에도 그런 꿈을 꾼 적이 있었니?"

스탠리가 그를 쳐다보았습니다. "그건 꿈이 아니라 . . . 그건 정말 일어났어요! 전 그냥 남과 다른 것에 지친 것 같아요, 제 생각에는."

레드필드 선생님이 자신의 손가락 끝을 함께 눌렀습니다. "다르다고? 네가 어떻게 다르다고 느껴지는지, 말해볼래?"

나쁜 시력과 안 좋은 기억력 둘 다 갖고 있으면서 어떻게 레드필드 선생님이 좋은 생활 지도 교사가 될 수 있는지 스탠리는 의아해했습니다.

"뭐, 전 제 학급에서 납작한 유일한 학생이니까요." 그가 말했습니다. "학교 전체에서 말이에요, 사실."

"흥미롭구나." 레드필드 선생님이 다른 메모를 했고 자신의 시계를 힐끗 보았습니다. "미안하지만 우리 시간이 다 되었구나, 스탠리. 넌 나를 다시 보기를 원하니? 그럼 그냥 엘리엇 선생님에게

알려 주렴."

"알았어요." 스탠리가 공손하게 말했지만, 그는 자신이 그럴 거라고 생각하지 않았습니다.

5장 왜 하필 나일까?

스탠리 형이 저녁 내내 슬퍼 보여, 라고 아서는 생각했습니다. 잘 시간이 되자, 그들이 누워서 램참 씨와 램참 부인이 잘 자라는 인사를 하러 오기를 기다리는 동안, 그는 자신의 형을 기운 나게 할 방법을 궁리했습니다.

비가 세차게 내리고 있었고, 그는 문득 스탠리가 간식으로 건포도를 먹었고, 아침이 되자 눈에 보이지 않게 되었던 비 오는 저녁을 기억했습니다. 날씨가 좋지 않을 때 과일을 먹는 행동에 대한 잘 알려지지 않은 결과라고, 댄 선생님은 설명했습니다.

"빗소리 들려, 스탠리 형?" 그가 말했습니다. "아무 과일도 먹지 않는 게 좋겠어."

"하, 하, 하." 스탠리의 말이 퉁명스럽게 들렸습니다. "그냥 날 내버려 둬, 응?"

"스탠리 형은 기분이 몹시 좋지 않아요." 아서가 램참 부부가 들어오자 말했습니다. "형은 심지어 저에게 말도 안 해

요."

"뭐가 문제니, 내 아들?" 램찹 씨가 물었습니다.

"아무것도 아니에요." 스탠리가 자기 머리 위로 그의 베개를 덮었습니다.

"만약 내 사진이 사실 거의 매일 신문에 실린다면, 나는 행복할 텐데." 아서가 말했습니다. "내 말은, 왜—"

램찹 부인이 그를 조용하게 했습니다. "스탠리, 얘야? 무엇이 너를 괴롭게 하는 거니?"

"아무것도. 아무것도 아니라니까요." 스탠리가 베개 밑에서 말했고, 일어나 앉았습니다. "하지만 왜 하필 저만 이래요? 왜 전 항상 납작해지거나, 눈에 보이지 않거나 그래야 하는 거예요? 왜 한 번이라도 그게 다른 사람일 수는 없는 건가요?"

"난 괜찮을 텐데, 정말." 아서가 말했습니다. "단지 한동안은 말이야. 난—"

"조용히 하렴, 아서!" 램찹 부인이 머리 위의 전등을 끄고, 구석에 있는 램프를 밝혔고, 그의 침대 위 스탠리 옆에 앉았습니다. 램찹 씨는 아서와 함께 앉았습니다. 부드럽게 창문에 떨어지는 빗소리, 작은 램프에서 나오는 은은한 불빛이 침실을 확실히 아늑하게 했습니다.

"난 네가 무엇을 말하는지 알겠구나, 스탠리." 램찹 씨가 마침내 말했습니다.

"왜 이런 일들이 너에게 일어나는 걸까? 네 엄마와 나도 그 답을 알지 못한단다. 하지만 일들은 종종 이유가 없는 것처럼 보이는데 일어나고, 그다음에 다른 무슨 일이 일어나면, 갑자기 처음에 일어난 일이 결국에는 어떤 목적이 있는 것으로 보이기도 하지."

"잘 말했어요, 조지!" 램찹 부인이 스탠리의 손을 꼭 잡았습니다. "우리가 아는 건 말이야, 사랑하는 스탠리, 우리는 너를 무척 자랑스럽게 여기고, 널 매우 사랑한다는 사실이란다. 그리고 우리는 납작해진 일, 그리고 그 모든 다른 예상치 못한 사건들이 얼마나 속상하게 하는지 이해한단다."

"정말로 그래요!" 스탠리가 말했습니다. "만약 엄마가 언제 납작해질지 전혀 모른다면 어떻게 하겠어요? 아니면 눈에 보이지 않으면요? 아마도 언젠가는 제가 10피트(약 3.05미터)만큼 자라거나 1인치(약 2.54센티미터)만큼 작아지거나, 아니면 초록색 머리카락이 생기거나, 혹은 꼬리가 달리거나, 그런 채로 일어날 수도 있잖아요!"

"그러게. . . ." 램찹 부인이 조용히 말했고, 램찹 씨가 와서 스탠리의 어깨를 쓰다듬었습니다. 그리고 그들은 두 아들 모두에게 키스해 주고는, 램프를 끄고 나갔습니다.

아서는 어두워진 방에다가 말했습니

다. "스탠리 형?"

"난 자려고 노력 중이야." 스탠리가 말했습니다. "뭔데?"

"나는 방금 생각하고 있었는데." 아서가 말했습니다. "만약 형이 눈에 보이지 않게 되고, 그다음에 납작해진다면, 사람들이 어떻게 알겠어?"

"허? 나는 모르겠—" 스탠리가 웃었습니다. "오, 그 말 이해했어! 납작해졌다는 것에 대해서 말이지. 좋은 농담이야, 아서."

아서도 또한 웃었습니다.

"조용히 해 줘, 부탁해." 스탠리가 말했습니다. "나는 자려고 하고 있다고."

"알았어." 아서가 말했지만, 그는 잠들기 전에 여러 번 낄낄거리며 웃었습니다.

6장 엠마

램찹 씨가 다음 날 오후 일찍 잔뜩 흥분해서, 집으로 돌아왔습니다.

"무슨 일이 있는지 맞춰 볼래요?" 그가 말했습니다. "그 시내에 있는 오래된 머커 백화점 있잖아요? 팔 층에, 모두 비워지고, 허물기를 기다리던 거? 뭐, 어젯밤에 그 대부분이 저절로 무너졌대요!" 그가 TV 뉴스를 틀었습니다. "최신 뉴스를 봅시다!"

". . . 머커 건물 붕괴에 대해 더 이야기해 보겠습니다!" 뉴스 진행자가 말하고 있었습니다. "그건 이제 단지 돌무더기에 불과합니다, 여러분! 세 명의 인부가 가벼운 타박상으로 치료를 받았지만, 다른 부상은 보고되지 않았습니다. 일반 사람들은 그 지역을 피해달라고 요청을 받았는데, 그 기간이—"

젊은 여자가 달려와서, 그에게 종이 한 장을 건넸고, 다시 달려 나갔습니다.

"잠깐만요! 이 소식이 방금 들어왔습니다!" 뉴스 진행자가 그 종이를 보고 읽었습니다. "와! 어린 소녀가 그 모든 잔해 밑에 갇혀 있다고 합니다! 엠마 윅스라는, 지역 사업가 오즈월드 윅스(Oswald Weeks)의 딸입니다!"

"엠마 윅스라고!" 스탠리가 외쳤습니다. "저 애는 저랑 같은 반이에요! 그녀가 오늘 학교에 오지 않은 게 당연하네요!"

"엠마는 다치지 않은 것으로 보입니다." 뉴스 진행자가 계속 말했습니다. "현장으로 출동한 소방관들은 잔해에 있는 작은 틈 사이로 그녀가 외치고, 음식과 물을 요구하는 소리를 들을 수 있답니다! 하지만 존슨(Johnson) 소방 서장은 그 어떠한 구조 활동도 금지했습니다! 모든 소란과, 잔해가 조금이라도 움직인다면, 그가 말하기를, 건물의 나머지를 무너지게 할 수 있다고 합니다!

이제, 여기 톰 밀러(Tom Miller)가 전합니다!"

TV 화면은 마이크를 든 기자가 무너진 건물 옆에 서 있는 걸 보여주었습니다.

"엠마 윅스!" 기자가 외치면서, 자신의 마이크를 틈에 가져갔습니다. "내 말이 들리나요? 괜찮나요?"

엠마의 목소리는 희미했지만 분명했습니다. "오, 그럼요! 전 정말 괜찮아요! 전 매일 건물이 제 위로 무너지기를 원했던 걸요, 당신도 알겠지만? 어서요, 저를 여기서 꺼내 줘요!"

램찹 부인이 한숨 쉬었습니다. "저런 불쾌한 어조라니! 그녀는 물론, 큰 압박감을 받고 있겠지만 말이야."

"엠마는 항상 저래요." 스탠리가 말했습니다.

30분 후에, 램찹 부인이 저녁을 준비하는 동안, 밖에서 사이렌 소리가 들리다가, 잦아들었습니다. 현관문을 열자, 램찹 씨는 소방서 차량이 연석에 있는 것을 보았습니다. 문간 계단 위에는 존슨 소방 서장과 무척 걱정스럽게 보이는 남자와 여자가 서 있었습니다.

"램찹 씨?" 존슨 서장이 말했습니다. "전 바로 본론을 이야기하겠습니다, 선생님. 전 당신이 어린 엠마 윅스에 대해 들어봤다고 생각해요, 그 머커 잔해에 갇힌 애 말이에요? 흠, 여기에 있는 윅스 부부 그리고 저, 우리는 여러분과 이야기를 나누고 싶습니다."

"물론이지요!" 램찹 씨는 손님을 집안으로 안내했고 그들을 자기 가족에게 소개했습니다.

"오, 윅스 부인!" 램찹 부인이 외쳤습니다. "당신의 가엾은 딸! 당신은 몹시 걱정되겠어요!"

"우리는 정말 걱정돼요!" 윅스 씨가 말했습니다. "하지만 존슨 서장은 당신의 스탠리가 엠마를 구할 수 있을 거라고 생각하고 있어요!"

"누구, 저요?" 그리고 "누가요, 스탠리 형이요?" 라고 스탠리와 아서가 말했습니다.

존슨 서장이 설명했습니다. "문제는 경찰관, 혹은 제 소방관 가운데 한 명이 안으로 길을 파서 엠마에게 가려고 한다면, 건물 나머지 전체가 그들 위로 무너질 수 있다는 겁니다! 우리에게 납작한 소방관이 없다니 정말 안됐어, 라고 전 생각하고 있었지요. 납작한 사람이라면 엠마가 부를 때 우리가 그걸 들을 수 있어서 거기 있다는 것을 아는 그 모든 좁은 구멍 사이로 비집고 들어갈 수 있을 텐데 말이에요. 그때 제가 여기에 있는 스탠리의 사진이 실린, 신문 기사를 기억했어요. 바로 저에게 생각이 떠올랐지요! 저 소년이라면 꿈틀꿈틀 움직여서 엠마에게 갈 수 있을 거라고!"

잠시, 모든 사람이 침묵했습니다. 그리고는 램찹 부인이 그녀의 고개를 저었습니다.

"그건 매우 위험하게 들리네요." 그녀가 말했습니다. "미안하지만, 전 안 된다고 말해야만 하겠어요."

"그건 조금 위험하기는 합니다, 부인." 존슨 서장이 말했습니다. "하지만 우리는 그 소년이 이미 납작하다는 걸 기억해야만 해요."

윅스 부인이 흐느꼈습니다. "오, 불쌍한 엠마! 우리는 어떻게 그녀를 구하죠?"

램찹 부인이 자신의 입술을 깨물었습니다.

스탠리가 무언가를 기억했습니다. "제가 그냥 생각해 보는 건데요." 그가 램찹 씨에게로 돌아섰습니다. "지난밤에 있잖아요? 제가 그 모든 말도 안 되는 일들이 계속 저에게 일어난다고 화가 났을 때 말이에요? 아빠가 뭐라고 말하셨는지 기억해요? 아빠가 때때로 아무도 이유를 알 수 없는 상황이 일어나고, 그리고 이후에 다른 어떤 일이 일어난다면, 갑자기 처음에 일어난 일이 결국에는 이유가 있는 것처럼 보인다고 하셨잖아요. 뭐, 제가 그냥 생각해보기에는, 제가 다시 납작해진 것이 어떤 말도 안 되는 일이고, 아마 그녀를 구하는 걸 시도해 볼 수 있는 유일한 사람이 저밖에

없는 곳에 엠마가 갇힌 것이, 그 두 번째 일일지도 모른다고요."

램찹 씨가 고개를 끄덕였고, 램찹 부인의 손을 잡았습니다. "우리는 우리 아들을 매우 자랑스럽게 생각해야겠어요, 해리엇."

램찹 부인이 잠시 생각했습니다. "스탠리." 그녀가 마침내 말했습니다. "너 저 거대한 건물이 네 위로 무너지지 않게 매우, 매우, 조심할 거니?"

"네. 그럴게요." 스탠리가 말했습니다.

램찹 부인이 윅스 부부를 돌아봤습니다. "우리는 스탠리가 돕는 것을 허락하겠어요." 그녀가 말했습니다. "그가 엠마를 위해 최선을 다할 거예요."

"여기가 훌륭한 남자아이가 있네요! 사자처럼 용감해요!" 존슨 서장이 외쳤습니다. "자 이제 들어봐요, 여러분! 램찹 부인, 당신은 제가 물건들을 준비하는 걸 도와줘요! 그리고 나서 스탠리가 엠마를 찾아 바로 들어갈 겁니다! 이해했나요? 지금부터 30분 후에, 모두 머커 건물 앞에서 우리와 만나요!"

7장 엠마, 너 어디에 있니?

늦은 오후의 햇살 아래, 오래된 머커 건물의 잔해 앞에서, 램찹 가족과 윅스 가족은 존슨 서장이 그의 구조 시도를 위

해 스탠리를 준비시키는 걸 지켜보았습니다. 데일리 센티널 사진기자, 플래시 토빈도 또한, 그곳에 있으면서, 사진을 찍었습니다.

램찹 부인은 빵과 치즈 두 장을, 각각 비닐에 싸서, 주었고 그녀의 할아버지의 납작한 은색 담배 상자에 포도 맛 탄산 음료를 채웠습니다. 존슨 서장은 빵과 치즈 상자를 스탠리의 팔과 다리에, 담배 상자는 그의 가슴에 테이프로 붙였고, 그에게 작고 납작한 손전등을 주었습니다.

그리고 그는 스탠리를 잔해에 난 큰 틈으로 데리고 갔습니다. "엠마!" 그가 외쳤습니다. "남자아이가 너를 구하러 갈 거란다! 그가 네 이름을 부르면, 넌 '여기!'하고 크게 외쳐서 그가 어느 방향으로 갈지 알 수 있게 해야 한단다. 알겠니?"

엠마의 목소리가 희미하게 나왔습니다. "네, 네! 서둘러요! 저 배고파 죽을 것 같아요!"

존슨 서장이 스탠리와 악수했습니다. "출발하렴, 얘야!"

저녁 햇살이 무너진 건물의 붉은 벽돌 위로 따스하게 빛나고 있었고 스탠리가 틈으로 가까이 다가갔습니다. 램찹 부인이 그에게 손을 흔들었고, 스탠리가 손을 흔들어 답했습니다. 그는 정말 잘 생겼어, 라고 그녀가 생각했습니다. 얼마나 용감하고, 얼마나 키가 크고, 얼마나 납작한지 몰라!

스탠리는 두 걸음 앞으로 걸어갔고 틈을 옆으로 지나가서 사라졌습니다. 잠시 후에 그들은 그의 외침을 듣게 되었습니다. "저기요(Hey)! 여기는 정말 어둡네요!"

"건초(Hay)는 말을 위한 거란다, 스탠리!" 램찹 부인이 답하며 외쳤습니다. "오, 신경 쓰지 마! 행운을 빈다, 애야!"

이곳은 그가 이제까지 알았던 어떤 곳보다도 훨씬 어두웠습니다. 스탠리는 그의 피부 위에 내려앉은 어둠을 거의 느낄 수 있을 정도였습니다. 그는 딸각 하고 자신의 손전등을 켰고 어려움 없이 앞으로 조금씩 나아갔지만, 그때 그 틈이 좁아지면서, 그를 느려지게 했습니다. 그의 왼쪽 다리 위에 있는 빵 조각이 무언가를 긁어, 그것을 붙이고 있는 테이프를 느슨하게 했습니다. 테이프를 다시 제자리에 누르면서, 그는 앞으로 꿈틀거리며 나가다가 막다른 길에 이르게 되었지만, 손전등을 조금 휘두르자 오른쪽과 왼쪽으로 갈라진 틈을 보았습니다.

"엠마?" 그가 불렀습니다.

"여기야!"

그녀의 목소리가 오른쪽에서 나왔고, 그래서 그는 그 갈라진 곳을 따라서 이

동했습니다. "엠마?"

"그래, 그래! 뭐야?"

"내가 네 이름을 부르면, 넌 '여기야'라고 말하기로 했잖아!"

"내가 이미 그랬잖아!"

그는 왼쪽으로 가는 다른 틈을 따라갔습니다. "엠마?"

아무 대답이 없었습니다. 스탠리는 몇 걸음 더 움직일 수 있었고 그때, 꽤 갑자기, 그 틈이 넓어졌습니다. 그는 다시 불렀습니다. "엠마?"

"바나나!"

"계속 말해." 그가 외쳤습니다. "난 네 목소리를 들어야만 한다고!"

"바나나! 여기야! 어쩌고저쩌고! 아무거나! 애, 나 네 불빛이 보여!"

그리고 그곳에 그녀가 있었습니다. 틈이 넓어지면서 작은 동굴이 되었고, 그 뒤편에 엠마가 앉아 있었습니다. 그녀의 청바지와 셔츠는 흙으로 더러워져 있었지만, 그의 불빛이 밝아서 눈을 가늘게 뜨고 있는 사람은, 거의 분명히 엠마였습니다.

"너!" 그녀가 외쳤습니다. "학교에 있는 애! 그 납작이!"

화를 내지 마, 스탠리가 자신에게 말했습니다. "난 사람들이 생각하기에 여기에 들어올 수 있는 유일한 사람이야. 기분이 어때, 엠마?"

엠마가 두 눈을 굴렸습니다. "오, 그냥 좋지 뭐야! 건물 전체가 내 위로 무너졌고, 사람들은 납작이를 보냈잖아! 그리고 지금 나는 배고파 죽을 것 같다고!"

스탠리가 빵과 치즈 조각을 떼어냈고, 그것들을 건네주었습니다.

"치즈야, 응?" 엠마가 자신의 샌드위치를 만들어서 한입 베어 물었습니다. "난 치즈를 싫어해. 마실 것 좀 있어, 납작이?"

"나를 납작이라고 부르지 마. 여기 있어." 그가 은색 담배 상자를 내밀었습니다.

엠마가 다시 자기 두 눈을 굴렸습니다. "난 담배를 피우면 안 돼."

"그건 탄산음료야."

그녀가 담배 상자를 열었고 조금씩 마셨습니다. "으웩! 난 포도 맛을 싫어해!"

존슨 서장의 목소리가 그녀 뒤에 있는 벽에 난 구멍을 통해서 나왔습니다. "스탠리? 너 거기에 도착했니?"

엠마가 엄지손가락으로 구멍을 휙 하고 가리켰습니다. "너를 부르잖아, 납작이."

"저 여기 있어요, 서장님!" 스탠리가 외쳤습니다. "엠마는 괜찮아요."

그는 환호 소리를 들었고, 다음에 서장의 목소리가 다시 들렸습니다. "나가는 길이 보이니, 스탠?"

“전 아직 살펴볼 기회가 없었어요. 엠마가 먹고 있거든요.”

“우리가 기다리마. 이상 끝, 스탠!”

“서장님도요!” 스탠리가 외쳤습니다.

그는 엠마가 그녀의 샌드위치를 다 먹을 때까지 기다렸습니다. “엠마, 너 어떻게 이런 엉망인 상황에 처하게 된 거야? 무엇 때문에 네가 여기에 오게 된 거야?”

“난 그냥 보러 왔을 뿐이야.” 엠마가 말했습니다. “그리고 사람들은 이 모든 안내판을 붙여 놨지! ‘위험! 들어가지 마시오!’ 사방에, 심지어 주차장 뒤에도 말이야. ‘들어가지 마시오! 위험! 위험!’ 나는 정말 그런 게 싫어, 알겠니? 그래서 거기에 이 문이 있었고, 그건 열려 있었지, 그래서 내가 안으로 들어갔어.” 그녀가 포도 맛 탄산음료를 다 마셨습니다. “좋아, 가자.”

“내가 들어왔던 길로는 안 돼.” 스탠리가 말했습니다. “난 간신히 비집고 들어올 수 있었어. 그리고 우리는 조심해야만 해, 왜냐하면—”

“나도 알아!” 엠마가 말을 잘랐습니다. “이름도 모르는 그 서장이라는 사람이 계속 내게 말했지: ‘움직이지 마! 나머지 건물 전체가 무너질지도 몰라!’ 그래서 나는 여기 아래에서 영원히 살란 말이야?”

“네가 들어왔다는 이 문 있잖아.” 스탠리가 말했습니다. “우리가 있는 이 동굴 같은 것을 찾기까지 얼마나 멀리 들어왔던 거야?”

“누가 멀다고 말하기라도 했니? 난 안으로 막 들어왔고, 이 요란하게 무너지는 소리가 났고, 건물 전체가 흔들리고 있었어, 그리고 난 바로 여기에서 넘어졌지! 요란한 소리가 영원히 이어졌어! 난 내가 죽는 줄 알았다고!”

“진정해.” 아이디어가 스탠리의 머릿속에 떠올랐습니다. “이 문이 정확히 어디에 있었어? 너 기억해?”

“저기 어딘가에 있었어.” 엠마가 그녀 뒤에 있는 어두운 구석을 가리켰습니다.

스탠리는 그의 전등을 휙 움직였지만, 단지 쪼개진 판자, 돌, 그리고 벽돌로 된 단단한 벽으로 보이는 것만을 보았습니다.

엠마가 조금 왼쪽으로 가리키다가, 오른쪽을 가리켰습니다. “아마 저기일지도 . . . 나도 몰라! 내가 사진이라도 찍든지 했어야 해? 그게 무슨 차이가 있겠어?”

“우리는 단지 그 문에서 조금 안쪽에 있을지도 몰라.” 스탠리가 말했습니다. “그리고 우리가 원하는 건 바로 그 밖으로 가는 거지.”

그 구석으로 더 가까이 다가가자, 그는 들쭉날쭉한 나무 조각이 허리 높이에 삐죽 튀어나온 것을 보았습니다. 그가 잡아당기자 그것이 쉽게 나오면서, 단단하지 않은 흙들이 따라 나왔습니다.

엠마가 그의 옆에 서 있었습니다. "너 왜 이렇게 엉망을 만드는 거야?"

그가 막대로 그 구멍을 쿡쿡 찔렀습니다. "아마 내가 찾을지도—"

흙이 벽에서 폭포처럼 쏟아지며, 그의 신발을 덮었습니다. 그는 이제 빛을 보게 되었는데, 그의 손전등에서 나온 작은 원형을 그리는 빛이 아니라, 햇빛이었습니다! 의심할 여지 없이 햇빛이었어요!

"오오오오!" 엠마가 말했습니다.

스탠리는 구멍을 더 크게 만들었고, 그들은 문이 구멍 바닥에 옆으로 놓여 있고, 잔해가 그 구멍 양옆으로 틈을 막고 있는 것을 보았습니다. 하지만 그건 충분히 컸습니다! 그들은 꿈틀거리며 지나갈 수 있을 것입니다! 그는 존슨 서장의 목소리가 들렸던 벽으로 다시 달려갔습니다.

"우리는 이제 나갈 거예요!" 그가 외쳤습니다. "우리는 뒤쪽, 안뜰로 갈 거에요!"

"알겠다!" 서장의 목소리가 들렸습니다. "잘했어!"

스탠리가 엠마에게 돌아섰습니다. "가자!"

"나는 온통 더러워질 거야." 엠마가 말했습니다. "우리는 아마 할 수—"

"어서!"

"소리 지르지 마!" 엠마가 말했지만, 그녀는 재빨리 구멍 사이로 기어갔고 스탠리가 바로 그녀의 뒤를 따랐습니다.

8장 영웅이다!

안뜰에서는 정말로 기분 좋은 광경이 펼쳐졌습니다. 램찹 부인은 스탠리와 아서에게 키스했습니다. 윅스 부인은 엠마에게 키스하고는, 다른 모든 사람에게도, 심지어 사진을 찍으려고 도착한 플래시 토빈에게도 입 맞춰 주었습니다. 램찹 씨는 윅스 씨와 존슨 서장과 악수했는데, 서장은 몇 차례나 스탠리가 훌륭한 영웅이라고 말했습니다.

플래시 토빈이 모든 램찹 가족이 있는 단체 사진을 찍었습니다. "한 장 더 필요해요." 그가 말했습니다. "엠마, 너와 스탠리만. 네 영웅이지, 그렇지? 네 목숨을 구했잖니!"

"전 혼자서도 나올 수 있었을 거예요." 엠마가 말했습니다. "전 단지 정확히 어디에 문이 있었는지 몰랐을 뿐이라고요." 하지만 그녀는 가서 스탠리 옆에 섰습니다.

"웃어!" 플래시 토빈이 사진을 찍었습

니다. "그래, 잘하고 있어!" 그가 스탠리의 등을 경쾌하게 찰싹 때렸고, 바로 그때 엠마의 팔꿈치가 스탠리의 갈비뼈를 세게 쿡 찔렀습니다.

"아야!" 스탠리가 소리 질렀습니다.

엠마가 환하게 미소 지었습니다. "너를 위한 거야, 내 영웅!"

"너 정신 나갔니? 뭐가—" 스탠리가 말을 멈췄습니다. 모든 사람이 그를 쳐다보고 있었습니다. 그는 이상한 기분이 들었는데, 마치—그래요! 그가 다시 둥그렇게 변했습니다!

"와!" 엠마가 말했습니다. "너 어떻게 그렇게 한 거야?"

"얘야, 너 정말 잘 됐구나!" 램찹 부인이 외쳤고 안뜰에 있던 다른 사람들에게서도 더 많은 외침이 나왔습니다. "내가 본 걸 너도 봤어? . . . 그가 부풀어 올랐잖아! . . . 우리가 미치기라고 한 거야?"

플래시 토빈이 다시 자신의 카메라를 겨누었습니다. "기다려, 얘야!"

하지만 그는 너무 늦었습니다. 그의 앞에는 이제 미소 짓는 스탠리 램찹이, 평범한 소년의 모습이 되어 서 있었거든요!

램찹 씨가 달려와서 그를 안아주었고, 다른 모든 사람이 박수를 보냈습니다.

"소방서에 30년이나 있었는데, 저런 것은 절대 본 적이 없어!" 존슨 서장이 말했습니다. "놓칠 수 없는 광경이야!"

"전 정말로 기뻐요." 스탠리가 말했습니다. "하지만 무엇이 그 일이 일어나게 했을까요?"

"댄 선생님이 말했던 대로야!" 아서가 외쳤습니다. "기억해요? 그 뼈가—어떻게 되고—그게 뭐든지 간에요!"

"OBP! 뼈 균형점이야." 램찹 씨가 미소 지었습니다. "그래! 플래시 토빈이 등을 때린 것, 그리고 엠마가 쿡 찌른 것! 그것 때문이야!"

머커 건물의 기울어진 지붕에서 판자가 빠져, 안뜰 구석에 떨어졌습니다.

"어서 갑시다, 여러분." 존슨 서장이 말했습니다. "우리는 여기에서 안전하지 않아요!"

잠시 뒤, 다시 거리로 나오자, 더 많은 포옹과 키스 그리고 잘 가라는 인사들이 오고 갔습니다. 갑자기, 그들 위에서, 큰 삐걱거리는 소리와 끼익 하는 소리가 들렸습니다. 돌아서서, 그들은 머커 건물에서 남아있던 것이 무너져 내리는 것을 지켜보았습니다.

엠마가 먼저 말했습니다. "오, 이런." 그녀가 조용히 말했습니다. "와!"

웍스 부인이 그녀의 눈길을 끌었고 스탠리를 향해 작게 고개를 끄덕였습니다.

엠마는 혼란스러워 보였습니다. "응?

. . . 오, 그래!" 그녀가 스탠리에게 돌아섰습니다. "난 아마도 네가, 있지, 내 목숨을 구한 것 같아. 어쨌거나 말이야." 그녀가 그의 뺨에 키스했습니다. "정말 고마워, 스탠리 램찹."

"괜찮아." 스탠리는 얼굴이 잔뜩 붉어져서, 말했습니다. "천만에."

모든 사람이 집으로 갔습니다.

9장 유명해지다

다음 날 저녁 잠자리에 들 시간에, 램찹 가족은 다시 그들이 그날 오전에 아침 식사를 하면서 정말로 읽는 것을 즐겼던 데일리 센티널을 다시 읽었습니다.

1면에는 표제가 이렇게 쓰여 있었습니다: 무례한 여자아이 구출되다! 납작한 구조자 형태를 되찾다! 그 아래에는 플래시 토빈이 찍은 두 장의 사진이 있었는데—램찹 가족사진과 엠마가 그의 갈비뼈를 찌르기 바로 직전에 찍힌 스탠리와 엠마 사진이었습니다. 아서는 특히 가족 사진에 흡족해했습니다.

"드디어!" 그가 말했습니다. "단지 스탠리 형만 나온 게 아니에요! 사람들은 그가 동생이 있는지 궁금해했을지도 몰라요, 그렇죠? 제가 이거 가져도 돼요?"

"그래도 된단다." 램찹 부인이 말했습니다. "난 엠마와 함께 있는 스탠리의 사진을 원한단다, 내 부엌 벽에 붙이기 위해서 말이야."

"전 사진 따위는 관심 없어요." 스탠리가 말했습니다. "전 단지 제가 다시 납작해지지 않기를 바랄 뿐이에요."

램찹 부인이 그의 손을 쓰다듬었습니다. "내가 네 회복에 대해서 댄 선생님에게 이야기했단다, 얘야. 그는 그 납작해지는 일이 다시 일어나는 게 거의 불가능하다고 생각한단다."

"좋았어!" 스탠리가 말했습니다.

아서는 신문에서 가족사진을 오려냈고, 빨간색 연필을 써서 그를 가리키는 화살표를, 아래에 있는 하얀 공간에, 그려 넣었습니다. 화살표 아래에, 그는 적었습니다, 영웅의 동생이라고 말이에요. 그리고 그는 그 사진을 자기 침대 위에 있는 벽에 테이프로 붙였습니다.

곧 모든 램찹 가족은 잠이 들었습니다.

끝

Chapter 1

1. B Mrs. Lambchop was making breakfast. Mr. Lambchop, at the kitchen table, helped by reading bits from the morning paper. "Here's an odd one, Harriet," he said. "There's a chicken in Sweden that rides a bike."

2. A While Stanley filled his backpack, Arthur bounced a tennis ball. "Let's go," he said. "Here! Catch!" Stanley had just reached for a book on the shelf by his bed. The ball struck his back as he turned, and he banged his shoulder on a corner of the shelf. "Ouch!" "Sorry," Arthur said. "But let's go, okay? You know how long—STANLEY!" "Why are you shouting?" Stanley adjusted his pack. "C'mon! I'm so hungry—" He paused. "Oh, boy! Arthur, do you see?" "I do, actually." Arthur swallowed hard. "You're, you know . . . flat."

3. A "The pump?" Stanley said. "It might work again." Arthur fetched the bicycle pump from their toy chest, and Stanley lay on his bed with the hose end in his mouth. Arthur gave a long, steady, pump. Stanley made a face. "That hurts!" Arthur pumped again, and Stanley snatched the hose from his mouth. "Owww! That really hurts! It wasn't like that before. We'd better stop."

4. D Mrs. Lambchop's call came again. "Boys! Please come!" "Do me a favor," Stanley said. "You tell them. Sort of get them ready, okay?"

5. D Stanley stood now beside Arthur in the doorway. "Just look." "Good grief!" said Mr. Lambchop. "I can't believe that bulletin board—" "It didn't fall on me this time," Stanley said.

Chapter 2

1. C "We are at a loss to account for this attack of flatness." "Hmmm." Dr. Dan thought for a moment. "Is there, perhaps, a family history of flatness?"

2. B He read aloud. "'Sudden flatness . . . extremely rare . . . minimal documentation . . . hearsay reports . . .' Ah, here it is! Dates back to the fifth century! 'During battle, Mongo the Fierce, an aide to Attila the Hun, was struck twice, simultaneously, from behind, and at once became no thicker than his shield. He became known as Mongo the Plate, and lived to old age without regaining his original girth.'"

3. D "The Osteal Balance Point may occur almost anywhere in the upper torso. It is vulnerable only to the application of simultaneous pressures at two points which vary depending on the age and particular 'design,' let us say, of the individual involved. In my opinion, the pressures created by the tennis ball and the shelf corner affected Stanley's OBP, thereby turning him flat."

4. A "The first time Stanley went flat, you were greatly puzzled by his condition," Mr. Lambchop said at last. "Now you seem remarkably well informed." "I read up on it," said Dr. Dan.

5. C At the door, Mrs. Lambchop turned. "Perhaps if we found the, you know, the OBP, we could make Stanley—" "No, no!" said Dr. Dan. "It would be dangerous to put the lad through such a skeletal strain again! And finding the OBP? Not very likely, I'm afraid."

Chapter 3

1. D "In this zip bag is another sail, called a spinnaker. We'll use that one for extra speed when we're running before the wind. See that boat way out there, how its spinnaker is puffing out front?"

2. A Mr. Jones pointed. "There! That's Jasper Green's boat, *Windswept*. He's the one I want especially to beat!" "Why? Are you mad at him?" Stanley asked. "He was very rude to me once."

3. B Stanley sat back, enjoying himself. The sun was bright, the breeze fresh against his face, the sky clear and blue, the water a beautiful slate color. There were boats on both sides of them, boats ahead, boats behind. How pretty they were, their white sails making cheerful crackling sounds as they billowed in the wind!

4. B Looking up, they saw that the top of the spinnaker had torn. *R-i-i-i-i-i-i-i-p!* The rip streaked downward, and now the spinnaker, torn all the way down, flapped uselessly in the wind. *Lovebug* slowed. "Drat!" Mr. Jones did his best with the mainsail. "Drat, drat, drat!" *Windswept* came up behind them. "Tough luck!" called Jasper Green. "Ha, ha!" "Drat!" Mr. Jones sighed. "Nothing we can do, Stanley. Unless— This may be crazy, but . . . Stanley, perhaps you could be our spinnaker?" "What?" Stanley shouted. "How?" "Good question," said Mr. Jones. "Let's see. . . . First, go take hold of the mast."

5. C Back in the clubhouse, Jasper Green would not admit that he had lost. A flat person used as a sail? He had never seen *that* before, he said, and went to the race committee office to complain. But he returned shortly to report that *Lovebug* had indeed won. The committee had advised him, he said, that there was no rule against a crew member allowing the wind to blow against him.

Chapter 4

1. A Only mean Emma Weeks was unpleasant. "Huh! Mr. Show-off again!" Emma said one day, but Stanley pretended not to hear.

2. D "I heard there was a flat kid here before," he said. "Helped catch sneak thieves at the Famous Museum of Art. But that kid, I heard he got round again." "It was me," Stanley told him. "You go back and forth, huh?" The photographer was impressed. "Okay, get round now. I'd like a shot of that too."

3. D There was a soccer team practice that afternoon, and the day was windy. It was worrisome, the coach said, the way Stanley got blown about. Perhaps, for the sake of the team, he should switch to an indoor sport.

4. B Miss Elliott, his homeroom teacher, noticed that he was not his usual cheerful self. "Mr. Redfield, the new guidance counselor, is said to be very helpful to troubled students," she told him. "I will ask him to find time for you."

5. B Mr. Redfield nodded. "This flatness, it's come upon you before, I'm told. Is it possible that somehow, without even admitting it to yourself, you wanted it to happen again?"

Chapter 5

1. C "Stanley's in a terrible mood," Arthur told Mr. and Mrs. Lambchop when

they came in. "He won't even talk to me."

2. A "But why me? Why am I always getting flat, or invisible or something? Why can't it just once be someone else?"

3. C "Why am I always getting flat, or invisible or something? Why can't it just once be someone else?" "I wouldn't mind, actually," Arthur said. "Just for a while."

4. B "I do see what you mean, Stanley," Mr. Lambchop said at last. "Why do these things happen to you? Your mother and I don't know the answer either. But things often happen without there seeming to be a reason, and then something else happens, and suddenly the first thing seems to have had a purpose after all."

5. B Mrs. Lambchop squeezed Stanley's hand. "What we do know, Stanley dear, is that we're very proud of you, and love you very much. And we understand about the flatness, and all the other unexpected happenings, how upsetting it must be."

Chapter 6

1. D Mr. Lambchop came home early the next afternoon, full of excitement. "Guess what?" he said. "The old Merker Department Store downtown? Eight floors, all emptied out, waiting to be torn down? Well, last night most of it fell down by itself!"

2. D "Emma's not hurt, it appears," the newscaster continued. "Firemen called to the scene can hear her calling up through chinks in the wreckage, demanding food and water! But Fire Chief Johnson has forbidden any rescue efforts! Any disturbance, any shifting of the wreckage, he says, might bring the rest of the building crashing down!"

3. C "Emma Weeks!" shouted the reporter, holding his microphone up to a crack. "Do you hear me? Are you all right?" Emma's voice was faint but clear. "Oh, sure! I'm just great! I hope a building falls on me every day, you know? C'mon, get me out of here!"

4. A Chief Johnson explained. "Problem is that if a policeman, or one of my firemen, tries to dig his way in to Emma, the whole rest of the building could crash down on 'em! Too bad we don't have a flat fireman, I was thinking. Flat fella could squeeze through all those narrow openings we know are there, 'cause we hear Emma when she calls. Then I recollected the newspaper story, with a picture of Stanley here. Hit me right away! *That* boy could maybe wiggle in to Emma!"

5. D For a moment, everyone was silent. Then Mrs. Lambchop shook her head. "It sounds terribly dangerous," she said. "I'm sorry, but I must say no."

Chapter 7

1. B "Emma?" "Yeah, yeah! What?" "When I say your name, you're supposed to say 'Here!'" "I already did that!" He followed another crack to the left. "Emma?" There was no answer. Stanley managed a few more feet and then, quite suddenly, the crack widened. He called again. "Emma?" "Bananas!" "Keep talking," he shouted. "I need to hear you!" "Bananas! Here! Blah, blah! Whatever!"

2. C "You!" she exclaimed. "From school! The flattie!" Don't lose your temper, Stanley told himself. "I was the only one they thought could get in here. How are you doing, Emma?" Emma rolled her eyes. "Oh, just great! A whole building falls on me, and they send in a flattie!"

3. D Stanley untaped the slices of bread and cheese, and handed them over. "Cheese, huh?" Emma put her sandwich together and took a bite. "I hate cheese. Got anything to drink, flattie?" "Please don't call me flattie. Here." He held out the silver cigarette case. Emma rolled her eyes again. "I'm not allowed to smoke." "It's soda." She opened the cigarette case and sipped. "Blaahh! I hate grape!"

4. B "Emma, how did you get into this mess? What made you come in here?" "I just came over to look," Emma said. "And they had all these signs! 'Danger! Keep out!' All over the place, even behind in the parking lot. 'Keep out! Danger!

Danger!' I really hate that, you know? So there was this door, and it was open, so I went in."

5. A Stanley made the hole still larger, and they saw that a door lay on its side across the bottom of the hole, wreckage limiting the opening on both sides. But it was big enough! They would be able to wiggle through! He ran back to the wall from which Chief Johnson's voice had come. "We're on our way out!" he shouted. "We'll be in back, in the courtyard!"

Chapter 8

1. A Flash Tobin took a group picture of all the Lambchops. "Need one more," he said. "Emma, just you and Stanley. Your hero, right? Saved your life!" "I could have got out by myself," Emma said. "I just didn't know exactly where the door was."

2. B Flash Tobin aimed his camera again. "Hold it, kid!" But he was too late. Before him now stood a smiling Stanley Lambchop, shaped like a regular boy! Mr. Lambchop ran to hug him, and everyone else applauded. "Been thirty years with the Fire Department, and never saw anything like that!" said Chief Johnson. "Wouldn't have missed it!"

3. D "I'm really glad," Stanley said. "But what made it happen?" "What Dr. Dan said!" shouted Arthur. "Remember? The Osteo-posteo-whatever!" "The OBP! The Osteal Balance Point." Mr. Lambchop smiled. "Yes! The slap on the back from Flash Tobin, and the poke from Emma! That did it!"

4. C A board fell from the tilting roof of the Merker Building, landing in a corner of the courtyard. "Let's go, folks," said Chief Johnson. "We're not safe here!"

5. A Turning, they watched what was left of the Merker building come crashing down. Emma spoke first. "Oh, boy," she said softly. "Wow!" Mrs. Weeks caught her eye, and gave a little nod toward Stanley. Emma looked puzzled. "Huh? . . . Oh, yeah!" She turned to Stanley. "I guess maybe you, you know, saved my life. Whatever." She kissed his cheek. "Thank you very much,

Stanley Lambchop."

Chapter 9

1. C At bedtime the next evening, the Lambchops read again the *Daily Sentinel* they had enjoyed so much at breakfast that morning.

2. C Arthur was particularly pleased with the family picture. "Finally!" he said. "Not just Stanley! People could have been wondering if he had a brother, you know?"

3. B "I don't care about pictures," Stanley said. "I just hope I never go back to being flat."

4. A Mrs. Lambchop patted his hand. "I told Dr. Dan of your recovery, dear. He thinks it most unlikely the flatness will occur again."

5. D Arthur cut the family picture out of the paper, and used a red pencil to draw an arrow, pointing up at him, in the white space at the bottom. Under the arrow, he wrote, *Hero's Brother*. Then he taped the picture to the wall above his bed.

Workbook text copyright © 2017 Longtail Books

스탠리, 다시 납작해지다!
(Stanley, Flat Again!)

1판 1쇄 2017년 9월 04일
2판 1쇄 2025년 9월 15일

지은이 Jeff Brown
기획 이수영
책임편집 김보경 정소이
콘텐츠제작및감수 롱테일 교육 연구소
저작권 홍하늘
마케팅 두잉글 사업본부

펴낸이 이수영
펴낸곳 롱테일북스
출판등록 제2015-000191호
주소 04033 서울특별시 마포구 양화로 113, 3층(서교동, 순홍빌딩)
전자메일 help@ltinc.net

이 도서는 대한민국에서 제작되었습니다.

ISBN 979-11-93992-42-5 14740